Thank You
DAVENTR
FOR THE
Memories.

FROM
ROCK 'N' ROLL
TO BEDPANS

LAWRENCE WHEELER

with special friends
NINA CASHMORE & MIKE TEBBITT

SUDDENLY...
PUBLISHING

This book is written to respectfully thank the people mentioned
and to honour their stories.

Editor - Joanna Clements
Publishing Director - Cheryl Thallon

First published in 2023
by Suddenly Publishing
15-17 High March
Daventry
Northants
NN11 4HB
UK

Copyright © Lawrence Wheeler 2023

All rights reserved. No part of this publication may be copied or reproduced
in any form without permission from the author or publisher.

The author, publisher and contributors are not responsible for any liability arising directly
or indirectly from the use or misuse of the information contained in this book.

A CIP catalogue record of this book is available from the British Library.

ISBN 978-1-739-34242-5

Printed and bound in the UK

Layout by Bee and Fox

To Jenny, Lisa and Alison
and generations to come

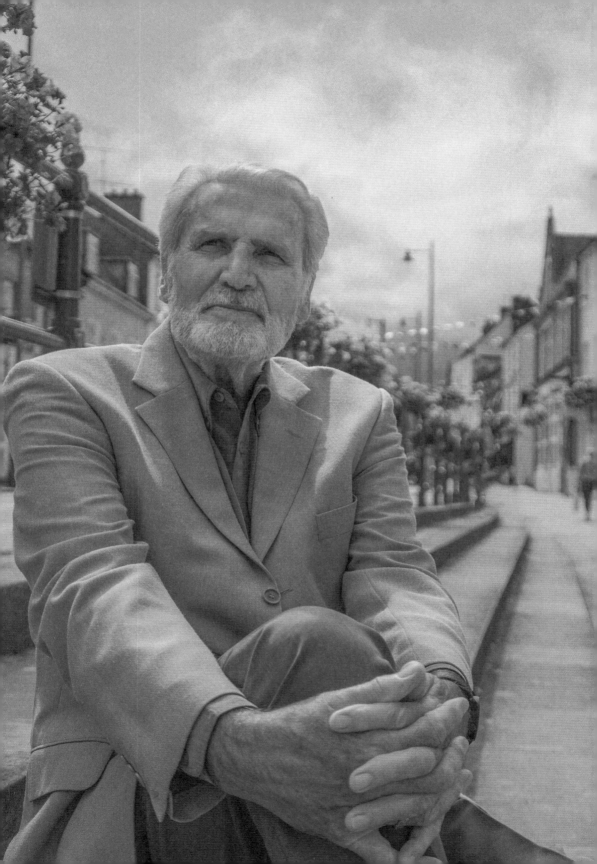

FOREWORD

"If only we both knew then what we both know now, we could have ruled the world," said Ian 'Ding' Davis to Lawrence at their first meeting.

"I first became aware of Lawrence in the late 1970s, while I was a DJ, entertainer and agent.

Lawrence was a staunch 'keep music live' evangelist and couldn't embrace the new-fangled Disc jockey phenomenon, so it would be a good while before we became friends. I finally became credible to Lawrence when I was made a Councillor of the Entertainments Agents Association GB in 1985.

Lawrence was King-of-the-Clubs when it came to booking top acts in those days and he was the first person I called when I was presenting an Entertainment Showcase at Wickstead Park in 1988.

We discovered a shared passion for cricket and eventually travelled together on several overseas cricket tours including Sri Lanka, the West Indies and meeting up in Australia at the Ashes in 2017,
over the years, we became firm friends."

Ian 'Ding' Davis F.E.A.A.

CONTENTS

INTRODUCTION

I'm delighted to bring my life story to print. *"From Rock 'n' Roll to Bedpans,"* my life over eight decades has been an adventure in and around the Daventry area working in the printing, newspaper, music, entertainment, hospitality and elderly care industries. Along the way, I developed a passionate interest in the stories and people of this historic market town.

In 2016, I started a Facebook page called 'Thank you Daventry... for the Memories'. I did this because Daventry has been wonderful for my family and myself, and it has given me so many opportunities. The idea of the page is for interested members to reminisce about the good old days in Daventry. At the time of writing (2023) there are around 9,000 members on the site, and I often get asked questions about my personal history, as many Daventry folk know of my involvement with local band, 'The Mavericks' and subsequently in the music and entertainment business and my association with the Wheatsheaf Hotel and Nursing Home, and other businesses in the town.

To bring added colour and historic detail to my memoir, I'm pleased to include contributions from my friends, local artist Nina Cashmore and ex-bookstore owner / former teacher, Mike Tibbett. I trust that you will find this collection of memories a warm and engaging read.

Thank you for buying this book, you are helping to raise some money for local charities. 100% of the cover price of this book will be donated to local charities. This has been made possible by the support of wonderful, local businesswoman, Cheryl Thallon, proprietor of the 'Sheaf Street Health Store' and the bookshop/publishing company 'Suddenly on Sheaf Street', to whom I am most grateful.

CHARITY BENEFICIARIES

The full cover price from the sale of this book will be donated to
and benefit the following local charities

Dem Cafe
www.demcafe.co.uk

DACT
www.dact.uk.com

The Air Ambulance
www.theairambulanceservice.org.uk

The New Street Café
www.daventryvolunteers.org.uk/our-projects/new-street-cafe

Daventry Food Bank
www.daventryfoodbank.org.uk

WHY A BOOK?

I WAS 61 years of age when I retired from business in 2004. I think that my wife Jenny was worried that I would be bored and have nothing to 'do', so she bought me a book called 'Writing Your Life Story'. She suggested that as I have had quite a lively and eventful life with various businesses and interests, I should put it in writing so that our children and grandchildren could understand a little more of where they came from and what has helped to make them who they are today.

Jenny and I were in the same class at school, although we did not become friends until after leaving Daventry County Modern School. I mainly became aware of Jenny when she would come to the 'Mavericks Club', a local music group which I was in on Monday nights at the Daventry Band Hall, so I suppose she was really a 'groupie' before they had their own title... only joking!

Without Jenny and the family's support, I would not have been able to follow the careers I have. As in all businesses and in life, there are always ups and downs, but I have been most fortunate with the support I have had from Jenny and our daughters Lisa and Alison.

I originally started this book about fifteen years ago in 2008, but for varying reasons, I am only just getting around to finishing it. I lost one copy when I was away on holiday in 2012 but restarted it later. It then got forgotten for a period, and then a few years ago, a very dear friend of ours Judith Stockil passed away, and it gave us both a jolt, and Jenny said 'if you are going to finish that book off, you had better do it before it is too late!'

Jenny and our daughters then bought me a super new computer for my 73rd birthday and told me that I then had no excuse not to finish the book, but again I lost the impetus, so as I have now reached the age of 80, I thought it is perhaps now or never!

THE EARLY YEARS IN BIRMINGHAM

I WAS BORN on the 2nd May 1943 to my mother Martha (Nellie) and father Ernest. I was the fourth child of the family, having two older brothers, Clive and Bryan, and a sister Iris. I was what was called a 'late' baby. This, I am reliably informed, was due to the one time in her life that my Mother drank alcohol... I think this explains a lot for my liking of the devil beverage in later life! Evidently, my Mom and Dad went on a weekend to Blackpool with their friends Bill and Wynn Pittaway, and my Mother, who was normally a non-drinker, got the worse for wear... too much information!

My parents were both born in Birmingham and my Dad worked all his life for British Timken, initially based at Aston, Birmingham. He was a chargehand in the Hardening shop and had to work – as did most folk in those days – very hard for his wages. I remember he would work Monday to Friday from 7.30am to 7.30pm, Saturday 8am to 4pm, and Sunday 8am to midday. This was a 60+ hour working week, in a very hot and manual environment. Because British Timken made bearings for tanks and planes etc., he did not have to go to fight in either of the wars, so we must be grateful for that. With four children to support, he had very little outside interest, apart from Aston Villa FC, whom he would take us to see when they played at home at Villa Park.

Our home was a three-bedroom council house, number 351 Kingstanding Road, Birmingham. My two older brothers and I shared one room, my sister had another and my Mother and Father had the third room. There was a kitchen and bathroom downstairs, along with a lounge and 'front room', this room was only used at Christmas or special occasions, or when either of my brothers were entertaining their lady friends. Young people now find it hard to believe that the 'front room' was just kept for 'special occasions'.

My oldest brother Clive was born in 1928, making him 15 years older than me. I can remember Clive always seemed to be in uniform. It was later explained that he was a member of the Cubs and Scouts groups, hence the uniforms. However, he did later do his National Service and served in the Army. This would be around the 1950s, I can remember that he served abroad a lot and it was always a great occasion when he came home 'on leave', when he would bring us all gifts. Photographs show that he was a dashingly handsome man, and I seem to recall many young ladies knocking on our front door when he was at home. On leaving the army he went to work for Reynolds Tubing in Birmingham, where he worked until he retired.

Clive married Mary in 1953. Mary was a nurse at Dudley Road Hospital and was nursing my sister Iris (more about this later) when they met. They went on to have two daughters – Jayne and Joanne, who have also married, and both have families of their own. Clive used to say that Jayne had many of my traits, and she has said to me many times that she is the 'black sheep of the family'. But she must have done something right, as she is happily married with two grown-up children and a business of several children's nurseries.

My other brother was called Bryan and he was born in 1931. He was a lovely man, very sensitive. Unfortunately, early in life he developed ear problems and had a mastoid in the ear. Consequently, he was not able to do National Service, so went straight to work after leaving school. He worked a short while at British Timken, but didn't like it, so moved to Alfred Roberts who dealt in rubber components. He worked there all his life. One of my memories of Bryan was that he was a beautiful piano player, and the only one out of all of us who kept up his lessons for playing the piano. Funnily enough, when we moved to Daventry in 1955, my Mother said whoever played the piano best, would have the family piano, which stood in the 'front room'. This was a 'no contest' as Bryan was the only one who had persevered and learned to play properly.

Bryan married his childhood sweetheart Georgina (Ena) and they had three children, Paul, Kim and Michelle. All have since married and have families. Sadly, Bryan died shortly after retiring in his mid-60s, after a long illness. We all miss him greatly.

Later, in 1955, when Mom, Dad and I moved to Daventry, Clive, Bryan and their families stayed in Birmingham, and have always lived around the Sutton Coldfield area.

The third child in our family was Iris, who was born in 1935. So, when I was born she would be eight years old. As I mentioned earlier, I arrived late and was spoilt by doting parents. I can remember that Iris and I clashed, but in speaking to others with older sisters, I think this often happens.

It is one of the saddest parts of my life that I never got to know my sister Iris better. Sadly, she contracted a kidney illness when she was fifteen and died at nineteen years of age. She was bed-ridden most of the time from her fifteenth birthday, and I know that my Mother never really got over her death for the rest of her life, and I think a lot of the mental health problems my mother had later in life, were brought on by the suffering and death she had to witness of her only daughter. I am sure these days they would have a medical cure or transplant available for my sister. But in the 1950s there were no such things available.

Towards the latter part of her young life, Iris's bed was brought down into the 'front room', so that she could be looked after and nursed better. As I mentioned earlier, Clive met Mary at the hospital when Iris was ill, and one of the last things that Iris was able to do before her death was to be a bridesmaid at Mary and Clive's wedding. She died shortly afterwards. Life seems so unfair when young people die. I hope that my children and grandchildren outlive Jenny and I, as I cannot think of anything worse than having to lose your child. I know it just about destroyed my Mother, I think that this is one of the reasons that my parents moved us to Daventry... to make a 'fresh start', and not live in the house with sad memories.

Although my sister's early death was very upsetting, there were also many happy times during my first twelve years of life, which were spent at Kingstanding Road, Birmingham.

I particularly treasure memories of playing cricket with my two older brothers in the entry at the side of the house. We would play for hours, and because I was the youngest I was allowed three 'goes' to every one of theirs. They would bowl the tennis ball under-arm to me, so that I stood a chance of hitting it, this was because I was so much younger than they were. This memory was brought back to me some years later when I was playing cricket in the garden with my grandson Jack. He got me 'out' with a faster ball, and said that I could 'have another go, because 'you are old'. I really laughed at this - it was as if history was repeating itself in reverse.

As I mentioned earlier, we were a 'Villa' family, and before I was taught the ABC or maths, I had to learn – like everyone else in the family – the names of the best Villa team ever – according to my Dad. Not only did we have to learn the eleven names, but we had to be able to recite them quicker than anyone else. I can still remember the names of the 1919-1920 Cup Winning side, it was: Hardy, Smart, Weston, Ducate, Barson, Moss, Wallace, Kirton, Walker, Stephenson and Dorrell. Villa won 1-0, and the goal-scorer was Kirton, who incidentally had a Newspaper shop opposite our house on Kingstanding Road. My Dad was in awe of him and the team.

Another family tie-in with the Villa is that my Grandfather – on my Mother's side - was working on the re-building of the new grandstand at Villa Park in the 1930s. He was at work when he collapsed and died at the bottom of the ladder, just before he started to climb. My Mother always said jokingly, that if he had waited five seconds, he would have been halfway up the ladder, and if he fell then we would have got a lot of insurance!... I think she was only joking?!

Mom and Dad were also interested in the game of baseball, which will seem a strange choice for a family in Birmingham, but you have to remember that there were a lot of American GIs still based in Great Britain, plus some who stayed behind after the war. There was a baseball league in Birmingham, and my family supported a team called the 'Cardinals', their top player being an American by the name of Vic Lambrett. My Dad used to play for the Cardinals on odd weekends when he wasn't working, and I can recall spending many Sunday afternoons in the parks watching him play.

Also, my brothers would take me to see Birmingham Speedway at the

Alexander Stadium in Perry Barr on many occasions. The local hero was Graham Warren in those days, and he went on to win the World Speedway Championship. I can also remember going to Athletic meetings there, as it was the 'home' track for the Birchfield Harriers, and they also held the AAA Championships (Amateur Athletics Association) on occasions at the track. If I also told you I saw a guy there named 'Jake the Peg' – who actually only had one leg – jump off a platform 50ft high, into a tub of water only 10ft deep, you wouldn't believe me, would you?... but he did!

My first school was Cranbourne Road, which was nice and handy, just being at the bottom of the Kingstanding Road. I don't remember too much about my early school days in Birmingham, as I was only four when I started. I did though have a really good friend who I grew up with in my early life, his name was Mervyn Winwood, and he lived at 70 Atlantic Road, which ran parallel with the Kingstanding Road. I was one month older than him, but we struck up an immediate friendship. Ironically Mervyn 'Muff" Winwood also moved into the musical entertainment business.

As well as going to school together Mervyn and I also joined the St. John's Church Choir, which we attended twice on Sundays. This was a very lucrative job on Saturdays when we would be paid a shilling a wedding (5p in modern money), which was quite a lot then for schoolboys. On a good Saturday, we could earn seven or eight shillings… we really thought we had it made. We were inseparable and spent many happy hours playing football and climbing in the local sandpits together. He also had an Uncle who worked at a firework factory, so November 5th was always very memorable!

I did go to see him a couple of times after moving. But what I didn't realise was that he would come back into my life much later, in a most unexpected way.

Mervyn you see had a younger brother called Steven (Stevie) Winwood. A few years later, in 1963, they formed the music group 'The Spencer Davis Group', and they had many hit records and became an enormous recording group, selling millions of singles and LPs. Stevie later left the group to start his solo career and is now one of the top world recording artists, and he regularly fills theatres and stadiums in America. Europe, and the UK on his tours. Perhaps if I had stopped in Birmingham, I might have been in his group… then again, probably not as there wouldn't have been room for two vocalists! Mervyn later left the group and joined Island Records as a musical director, and produced many hit records including music by Bob Marley, and had one of the most successful records of the 80s, but I will get back to that later.

Like most 'old folk' now, my memories are limited about the first twelve years of my life, and although my parents were from large families, I can only remember a few of my Aunties and Uncles. On my Mother's side, there was Auntie Doll and Uncle Bert, who I can recall had emigrated to Australia in the late 1920s and had returned to England in the 1940s. They seemed a lovely couple, stop here for a thought… if my Mom and Dad had gone with them? I could have been born an Aussie!!!

Another Auntie and Uncle on Dad's side of the family were Florrie and Bert. What I remember most about them was that my Uncle Bert performed locally around Birmingham as a magician, and I can recall watching him perform, with my sister Iris as his assistant. She would have been about twelve or thirteen then, and it was before she was struck down with her kidney illness. I wonder if this is where I got my first taste of the entertainment world. If it was… thank you Uncle Bert.

The closest Auntie and Uncle to me, were Auntie Ivy and Uncle Bert who also moved to Daventry from Birmingham with British Timken. Auntie Ivy was a sister of my father, and we were very close. They lived in their own house in Wylie Road in Aston, Birmingham. As they had no children – and I was the youngest of my family – they really looked forward to my visits on Sunday afternoons. They would spoil me with treacle sandwiches and cream cakes, and we would watch children's TV together. Programs like 'Muffin the Mule' and 'Whirlygig'. They were called our 'rich Auntie and Uncle', mainly because they had no children, and owned two houses. But truthfully when they moved to Daventry they sold the two houses in Birmingham for a total of under £1,000 for the two, but money had more worth then.

Three other memories before I move on to the next part of my life. One was the Queen Elizabeth II Coronation in June 1953. Although I was only ten, I can remember it was a fantastic occasion. There were street parties, fancy dress and children's sports races. There were a few families with televisions (not us), so we were able to go in and watch the pageantry on neighbours' black and white televisions. At the time of finishing this 'Memory Book' in 2023, the Queen passed away last year, and her senior son Charles has been crowned King Charles III in May, 2023.

This was also the year 1953 of the 'Matthews Cup Final' at Wembley, when his football team Blackpool played Bolton in the final. Anyone who followed football knew of Stanley Matthews, probably one of the greatest England players of all time, and in the 50s was without parallel. He had played in two other losing finals, and this was to be his last chance of a winner's medal. They were losing the final 1-3, but with the magic of Matthews managed to turn the result around and they won 4-3. Although the game is remembered as the 'Matthews Final', another hero was Stan Mortenson, the Blackpool centre forward who scored a hat-trick for Blackpool in their victory. Our paths crossed many times later in life on the 'After Dinner' speaking circuit. He was a very modest man.

I will leave this period on – what I think is – an amusing note… first I have to explain that my Mother was a gardening fanatic, and I think she had the best turfed lawn outside of Wembley. Our garden in Birmingham was quite big for a council house, which they tended to be in those days. When we were moving to Daventry, my Mother couldn't bear the thought of leaving her beautiful lawn, so when we knew we were moving she arranged with a local garden centre to come and dig it all up and put it in rolls, there were dozens and dozens of them! She had it moved to Daventry and eventually had it re-laid after a very bad winter in our garden at 51 Tennyson Road. The turf took, and it is still in the garden of our old house. I often wondered what the family who moved into our Birmingham house thought. They would have been welcomed by a large sea of mud… I suppose we could put this down to my Mother's eccentricity!

MOVING TO DAVENTRY - SCHOOL AND MY TEEN YEARS

I WAS 12 YEARS of age when we moved to Daventry in 1955, my Mom, Dad and I moved into 51 Tennyson Road. My two brothers and their wives stayed in Birmingham. My father worked for British Timken at Aston in Birmingham, and when he was offered a move to Daventry, my Mom and Dad decided to take it. As my sister Iris had died recently, I think they thought a 'fresh start' in Daventry would be good for all of us.

British Timken were an American-based company with factories in the UK. They decided to close down the Aston factory in Birmingham and offered their employees jobs in the new factory in Daventry. At this time Daventry was a small market town of about 5,000 population (it is now around 30,000+ and expected to reach 40,000 over the next twelve years). It was steeped in history and being a market town its main interest was agriculture and making leatherwear like shoes and whips. I can always remember Market Day when cattle were brought from all over the country to Daventry – which is close to being in the centre of England. History books show that in the 1600s farmers would walk their cattle and sheep from as far as Wales to sell at the Daventry market, which was held at the Wheatsheaf Hotel in Sheaf Street (you will find the Wheatsheaf was a big part in my life, more of that later).

Daventry had more pubs to the square meter (or yards as it was then) than any other town in the Midlands. There were over 40+ licensed premises in the town in the 1800s!

British Timken Ltd had bought the site for the factory for £1.00 from the local district council, as they anticipated - quite rightly - that the Timken factory would bring plenty of new jobs to this 'overspill' town. Lots of houses were built on the Headlands estate, and our family were in the first ten houses released to British Timken in Tennyson Road. We were initially treated as 'outsiders' but after 60+ years of living here I feel more like a Daventrian than a Brummie.

After failing my 11+ exam, I initially went to St James School, in St James Street, Daventry. I did no more than a couple of terms there, and then we were moved to a brand-new school named Daventry Secondary Modern School, Ashby Road (later William Parker School, and now Daventry Parker E-Act Academy) for the next few years until I was 15. I was not outstanding in schooling.

I did though have a work ethic, which I think was of benefit later in life. I had four part-time jobs at the same time while under 15 years of age, and still at school. I would deliver newspapers every evening in Daventry and Drayton, and I would also make deliveries for Melias Grocery store in the High Street on Friday evenings and Saturdays, on one of those bikes with room for a big basket on the front. I also worked two evenings a week in the projection room at the Regal Cinema, where I had to change the film reels. Each reel lasted for 20 minutes and there were two projection cameras next to each other. You had to time it perfectly to get the one reel started, just as the previous reel finished. If you didn't you had that horrible period where there was a lot of grey flashing lights and darkness on the screen, before the next reel started. The pay was good at 6 shillings a night, plus you saw the films for free. I was also working Saturday mornings at the Daventry Weekly Express Newspaper, this was for six months before I left school and started a six-year apprenticeship there.

Fortunately, I was very sports-orientated, and as well as playing cricket and sprinting in athletics for the county, my main talent was football, in which I played in goal. I can recall that on my school report, where I had finished in my usual mid-table position, the teacher had noted on my exam report that I was 'not in the top level educationally, but should be successful playing football'. My Mother went berserk and came to the school and challenged the teacher who had written this, to prove to her how anyone makes a living from football... it is certainly a bit different now.

I was picked first for the South Northants school team and then was picked for the Northampton County School team. I was told that a selector for the England schoolboys team was coming down to Daventry to see me play at Stead & Simpson* sports ground against Derby schoolboys team. Unfortunately, on the Thursday before the Saturday, my Mother gave me a letter to post at the post box at Clare Avenue, so I got on my bike and set off, accidentally taking a corner a bit tight along Dryden Avenue I fell off and gauged my knee, the scar of which is still with me. The selector still came down to the game, and took me to one side and told me to get fit and they would have another look. Unfortunately, I was leaving school six months later, so that was not going to happen.

I was, however, approached by Northampton Town FC (the Cobblers) and I moved there to play for them for two seasons. Usually, apprentice players were given a job at a local builders so they could be released for training a couple of days a week. But I had already arranged an apprenticeship at Daventry Weekly Express, which I said I wanted to honour, so they accepted and allowed me to continue my apprenticeship at Daventry. I mainly played in the youth side but did get into the reserve side on a few occasions, but there were two established goalkeepers there at the time named Norman Coe and Gary Isaacs who held the main first and reserve team positions. I recall my reserve team debut at Luton Town, where I saved two penalties, but they made them take the second one again and they scored, we lost 2-1. Later Dave Bowen became manager and offered five of us young ones semi-professional forms. As I was well into my printing apprenticeship, and singing in the 'Mavericks' group then, I turned it down.

I also recall we drew Birmingham City in the FA Youth Cup on two consecutive seasons. We lost at home, and the following year lost at St. Andrews. After a toe injury, I moved to Rugby Town for half a season. I did play later for my beloved Daventry Town and Dun Cow, but that was mainly in an outfield position and just for fun, though you will see that injuries received during these games indirectly affected my life.

Unfortunately, due to working with small type and print, my eyes were deteriorating and being a goalkeeper that is not good. I must have had one of the very first sets of contact lenses. I recall they were made of thick glass, and in the first game I wore them, they cut into the lower lid of my eye. I went off to get the blood removed and was booked by the referee for leaving the pitch without permission. This was the first and only time in my career that I had been booked or sent off. Fortunately, I appealed to the Northampton Football Association, and it was overturned.

At this time I was also singing in 'The Mavericks', so I would be out most nights either playing in the group, or training with the Cobblers, flying here and there on my Vespa reliable scooter.

I shouldn't overlook that Jenny and I were now going 'steady'… what a quaint term, and she was getting used to my life in the entertainment industry and understood some of the benefits and problems of it!

*The Stead and Simpson Shoe Factory was a dominant manufacturer in Daventry from around 1880 until they were taken over by Whites in the 1970s. The factory was demolished in 1999 and the site redeveloped to construct the current Tesco supermarket in the town centre. The Stead & Simpson sports ground was located off what is now Eastern Way in the approximate area of where Norton Close now sits.

MY EARLY WORKING LIFE

WHEN I LEFT school at 15 years of age, and not knowing what I really wanted to do, I had seen an advert in the Daventry Weekly Express for a 'Printing Apprentice'. This entailed a six-year apprenticeship. I had not even been aware that there was a newspaper in Daventry, and certainly never read it. Later I was to learn that the advert for a 'Printing Apprentice' had been displayed for around eighteen months, but no one seemed to like the proprietor/editor of the newspaper Walter Green, whereas my parents or myself had never heard of him or the Daventry Weekly Express newspaper before.

I went for the interview and came into contact for the first time with Walter Green. He was a brilliant man and would write all the articles in the Daventry Weekly Express newspaper, set up the type, and would – along with the two or three staff employed - fold the printed newspapers and interleave them on Thursday nights, which was the printing night then. He would then deliver them, sometimes as late as 3am on Friday mornings, to the local newsagents for selling, so they had them for when their shops opened. In those days the circulation was around 2,500 copies. As well as the weekly publication, it was also a 'general printers', covering all types of printing items, from brochures to wedding invitations etc. The staff of the 'Gusher'*, as the newspaper was known locally, consisted of an elderly gentleman Alec Beech who was nearing retirement, one other apprentice and Mr Green.

Walter Green was a giant of a man, about 6ft 3in tall, and about 20 stone in weight. He was both intimidating while also genteel. He sacked me one Thursday night, after about a month, as I told him I was not prepared for him to speak to me the same way as he spoke to the other apprentice. He sacked me there and then and gave me two weeks' notice, but this was forgotten by the next day, and neither of us mentioned it again. I feel that there was a 'special bond' between Mr Green and myself. He suffered from epilepsy, and would frequently have bad 'turns'. I was often called up to his office to help move him to a more comfortable position. He was a big man to move.

I completed my six-year apprenticeship in August 1964 and coincidentally, got married to Jenny on the very next day. In fact, when writing a report on the wedding in the 'Gusher' the following week, Mr Green's headline for the wedding was: 'Fledged and Pledged'.

Soon afterwards Mr Green was sued by a schoolteacher at Ashby Road School named Mr Maurice Hill. As well as being a teacher at the school Mr Hill also arranged evening adult night classes. As I recall a class had to have twelve attending to fill the requirement for an evening class, and thereby Mr Hill would receive his bonus for arranging it. Unfortunately, there was a class for 'Eskimo Folk Law' which had a debateable number attending. Mr Green inferred in the newspaper that Mr Hill benefitted financially from this. He was then charged directly by Mr Hill with libel. This went to court in Northampton, and the case lasted three days. On completion, Mr Green was found guilty, but the judge awarded Mr Hill just 'one penny' damages, which Mr Green claimed was a victory for him. Unfortunately, the Judge awarded Mr Hill the costs, which totalled thousands of pounds. Money which stretched the Company's finances and made it difficult to continue with the paper.

Very soon afterwards I was 'tipped off' by Alec Beech that Mr Green was looking to sell the business, so I thought it best to move away before I was given my notice. So, I rang the Rugby Advertiser newspaper and asked them if they had any linotype jobs going. The linotype was a machine that set the hot metal type, and which I had learned to operate during my apprenticeship. They informed me that they had no vacancies for a linotype operator, but their sister company the Leamington Spa Courier were looking for one. So, I rang them and they offered me the job, which I accepted and spent nine years there, more details about this later.

Ironically after I had been there a couple of years the Leamington Courier Press Company bought both the Rugby Advertiser and the Daventry Weekly

Express themselves and moved the printing of both these newspapers to Leamington. So, I would have ended up there anyway, but having been there for two years already I was well established and had a good job.

Incidentally, after a few years, they advertised internally for someone to learn first aid to deal with any accidents that happened in the factory. I thought it would be interesting to learn first aid and it also meant I got paid 50p a week extra in that position. Generally, accidents seemed to be little finger cuts and the like. Except I recall that one afternoon I had to go to a family function, so I did not make it to work that afternoon. As it happened one of the gents who operated the big newspaper printing machine got his arm caught in the printer and it ripped his arm off. I am pretty sure I would have fainted if I had had to treat him!

In the meantime, my entertainment agency Falcon Management (later Lawrence Wheeler Agency) was expanding all the time and I was making a better financial return from the Agency than the wage at Leamington. I had though always said that I would not depend on other people's ability, which as an agent you do. Then playing football on a Sunday for the Dun Cow FC, I broke both my legs on different occasions in an 18-month period playing, so I had two four-month breaks (so to speak) from work when I couldn't drive to Leamington, so I worked on my Agency from home, and greatly increased the turnover further.

It is ironic that Mr Green and my path should cross again later in life when I was involved with the Wheatsheaf Nursing Home. I was away on holiday at the time, and when I rang back to the Wheatsheaf one day to double-check that everything was OK, they informed me that 'someone I knew had been admitted as a resident', on checking I learned that it was Mr Green. When I arrived back in Daventry, unfortunately, he had passed away. In a way I was very sorry not to have been able to say farewell to such an important man in my life, but on reflection, it was perhaps better for me to remember him as he was, a tall commanding man. Rest in peace Mr G.

*The Daventry Weekly Express was affectionately known as The Gusher to readers which harks back to when Daventry had a railway station (in Station Close behind McDonalds) and after a pre-WW2 train which reputedly never exceeded 5 miles an hour up the slight gradient between Daventry and Weedon – and was ironically dubbed the Daventry Express. This 'speedy' train apparently filled the surrounding countryside with fumes and smoke as it struggled up the hill, hence the nickname 'Gusher'.

Left: My daughters Lisa and Alison aged 5 and 3 years

Left: Lisa and Alison at Alison's wedding in 2004

Left: Wheeler Family at home in 2013

Below Back row: my Father, Mother,
Auntie Ivy and Uncle Bert.
Below front row: Clive, Iris and Bryan.
Below front left photo: Clive, myself and Bryan.
Below front right photo: Mom and Dad later in life

Above: The Wheeler Family at Bourton on the Water, one
of our favourite places. This was when the family took
Jenny and I to celebrate our 80th birthdays

Above: Mom, Dad and myself
enjoying a holiday in Jersey

Above: The Spencer Davis group, of which Mervyn *(on left)* was
a member, along with younger brother Steve Winwood *(on right)*
who has become a world-renowned artist

Above: Daventry County Modern football team 1957/58

Above: 'The Mavericks' band.
Back row: Ray Howes *(left)* and Ken Ballinger *(right)*.
Front row: Stan Fonge *(left)* and Terry Ballinger *(Right)*. Oh Yes, that is me in the middle wearing my "Pink Suit"! in approx. 1959

Above: 'The Mavericks' performing in the early 1960s at Stead and Simpson summer fete, one member short due to illness

Above: 'The Mavericks' reunion in mid 1980s at British Timken Social Club

Left: Walter Green, the Proprietor/ Editor of the Daventry Weekly Express newspaper. He became like a father figure to me, after initial problems

ENJOYING SPORT

I HAD ALWAYS been interested in football, and as I mentioned earlier in the book my Father and brothers were staunch Aston Villa fans, and they would take me to the 'Villa' home matches when we lived in Birmingham to support the team. I remember when I first came to Daventry when I was 12 years of age I immediately 'fell in love' with Daventry Town FC when I went to a Cup Final at Dunchurch in 1955 and saw them win 1-0. To this day I have always supported them, and I became Chairman in the mid-1980s for a time.

In Birmingham, I went to Cranbourne Road School and because I was the tallest in the class I was made the goalkeeper. I recall in my first game I dropped the ball out of my hands to kick it and managed to kick it over my own head. I remember we lost the game 6-0. When we moved to Daventry I went to the County Modern School on Ashby Road and continued playing in goal, but getting a little better. I did get picked for the school South Northants team along with a friend from Braunston named Richard Barnwell. We were then picked for the Northampton County team who played in a national school championship.

Shortly before leaving school I was approached by Northampton Town FC to sign and play for them in the Youth side which I did for a couple of seasons, and played in the FA Youth Cup twice at Birmingham City. I recall that the home game against Birmingham was the only time my Father had watched me play, which is sad really, but he died when I was only nineteen years of age. Richard Barnwell who was a good friend, and later was my 'Best Man' when Jenny and I got married. He signed on for Coventry City at the same time.

I played mainly in the Youth side at the 'Cobblers' being sixteen years of age, though I did get in the Reserve team on occasions playing in the Football

Combination league, when one of the two first choice goalkeepers were injured or not available. Then the reserve games were sometimes played at major football grounds.

It was my fault that I left Northampton Town. Having gone to work at the Daventry Weekly Express I was handling small print type and it began affecting my vision. I was offered a job at a building company, which was owned by a director of Northampton Town FC. Young players were given jobs there which left them free on Tuesday and Thursday mornings to go for training with the first team and reserve squads. But I had taken an apprenticeship with Walter Green at the Daventry Weekly Express, and I wanted to continue with that. Eventually, a toe injury kept me out of the team for a while, and in the meantime, I had joined 'The Mavericks' music group which was a turning point in my life.

During that time, I had started playing for Daventry Town FC on occasions when I wasn't required at Northampton Town, but as Daventry Town had a regular goalkeeper I played on the field just to keep fit. This was the start of my relationship with Daventry Town FC which I still treasure to this day, I still support and follow them home and away. I have had this affection for them for going on for more than sixty-five years. I remember when I used to play for them in the early days, I would on occasions shoot off immediately after a game, on my Vespa scooter to perform with 'The Mavericks' group even without having a shower. Getting changed in the theatre dressing room later, my knees would be covered in mud from the afternoon's game.

As mentioned earlier Daventry Town FC has become a big part of my life over the years, and nowadays I go to watch them play regularly with two fellow supporters, writer and former history school teacher Mike Tebbitt, and a good friend Jim Henderson.

I have always enjoyed sport and travelled to Australia and South Africa with my good friend Richard Stockil who played cricket for Captain Hawkins XI, from Everdon, for many years. The slightly eccentric Captain Hawkins would only play away games abroad, hence tours to Australia and South Africa. Being an old English gentleman, he was always made a 'fuss' of by the teams they played. I had really only gone on the tours for the 'ride', but I did play on a couple of occasions to give some of the touring players a rest. Occasionally teams touring from abroad would play at Everdon, and just loved the typical English setting.

I also went to the Bahamas with the Wellingborough Rugby team. Another friend Robin Leslie, who played for them, rang me up one day and told me that someone had dropped out of this tour, and there was a place available. I had never been to the Bahamas, so took the opportunity. I was forty years of age at the time and had never played Rugby. It was a great tour, but I was told when they reached the last fixture that I was expected to play as all tourists had to play at least one game. So, I turned out in the team and got completely overrun. It was far too rough for me.

I still enjoy watching England cricket team and Test cricket and have been fortunate to see them play Test matches against most of the cricketing countries.

BREAKING INTO SHOW BUSINESS

I HAVE BEEN asked many times over the years, how the Lawrence Wheeler Agency was started, and what made me become an agent in the first place. So here is the story, from the most unlikely beginning...

It really all began in 1958 when I was 15 years of age and in my last year at Daventry County Modern School. I was due to leave in the summer, and I had an apprenticeship lined up at the Daventry Weekly Express in the printing department. At the time I was also a keen goalkeeper and played for the school side, and the Northants County side as mentioned earlier.

As Christmas approached in my last year at school, one of the teachers decided he wanted to put on a Christmas show featuring the school classes. So, somehow or other, it was decided that four of us young lads would form a vocal quartet, which we did, and we called ourselves (modestly) 'The Fabulous Satellites', this consisted of Alan Matthews, Stan Fonge, Chas Reynolds and myself. We wore black trousers, white shirts, dickie bows and black shoes. We then MIMED to three 'Ink Spots' records. Yes, we didn't actually sing, just mimed. Incidentally for younger readers, the 'Ink Spots' were a four-piece vocal act very popular at the time. Our songs went down very well, and there was lots of applause and cheering, I think that was the start of my love affair with entertainment. Incidentally miming is now called lip-syncing, but I think it is equally as bad!

About a year later, after leaving school, I was walking along the High Street in Daventry and met Stan Fonge for the first time since leaving school. We chatted, and I asked him what he was doing with himself, and he told me he had started playing the drums and had joined a pop group 'The Mavericks', who were established locally and consisted of Ken and Terry Ballinger, Ray Howes and himself, plus a vocalist. He said the vocalist wasn't very good, and that I should audition for the group. Bearing in mind the only performing I had done was miming/lip-syncing at school, I said OK and went along for an audition at Weedon. Before I started, they told me they were looking for a vocalist who would move about the stage, i.e. like Elvis and Cliff etc., and with this in mind, I threw myself about (helped having been a goalkeeper I suppose) and got the job.

For the next two plus years, it was great, we had quite a following around the Midlands in particular. We would do town hall and village hall gigs on Friday and Saturday nights and appear on the Granada Theatre circuit on Sunday nights (2 x 20 min spots between films). On Mondays, we would have the 'Mavericks Club' at the Band Hall in Daventry. This building is no longer there, but was located roughly opposite the current Waterloo Car Park off Warwick Street. Tuesday nights would be at the Whilton Hall in Bletchley and then we would rehearse on either a Wednesday or Thursday evening to learn new songs. Terry and Ken's Dad would transport us around, and a lad named Dave Norrie would 'roadie' for us. I would be training on Thursday nights at Northampton Town FC, so I had a very busy life in those days and I had a Vespa scooter to get around on.

'The Mavericks' had a good following, and along with a local group from Banbury called Paul Gadd and the Ravens, were always in demand locally. Paul Gadd later changed his name to Paul Raven and released a cover version of 'Green Door' which was a hit song for Frankie Vaughan. He then changed his name again to Gary Glitter… and the rest, as they say, is history!

We tended to do two types of 'gigs': either a dance night or a cabaret show. Cabaret shows were mainly on Sunday nights and the performance and presentation were more important as you were playing to a seated audience.

I cringe now, when I am not smiling, as at those shows I used to wear a pink brocade suit, black shirt, white tie and white cricket boots! Yes, that is right, I couldn't get white shoes in size 11 those days, so I had to wear cricket boots with the studs taken out.

The pink suit was specially made by a little suit tailor down Bridge Street in Northampton. It was quite expensive at the time, around £28.00. I recall that when we opened our cabaret show, I would start with the Elvis song from the King Creole film, 'If you are looking for trouble, you've come to the right place'. You can imagine the reaction I would get these days performing in a pink brocade suit and asking 'If you are looking for trouble?' But they were good days, times were different.

As invariably happens, there was a break-up in the group after about two years, and when I was 19 I left the group to be replaced by a local female vocalist Pauline Bliss and a male vocalist Johnny Gold. I won't go into the reason for leaving but suffice to say that it was a petty argument, and I still remain friends with all former group members. In fact, the late Ray Howes and his wife Shirley, and myself and Jenny used to meet every month for a get-together and holiday at least twice a year together. Ray liked a drink (like me), and our wives didn't drink, so it worked out perfectly!

We did all get back together in 1987 for some reunion shows on the 25th anniversary of the forming of the original group in the 1960s. The idea for our reunion came from Ray, who was the Works Manager at British Timken in Daventry, where I used to put on monthly cabaret shows through the Agency. He suggested, one day when we were having a drink, that we all got back together for some shows. So we booked a Friday, Saturday and Sunday night one weekend at the Daventry British Timken Social Club, and raised money for charity. The tickets sold out quickly, and we had excellent support acts. The shows were so successful that we decided to do a run of three more shows in October. Again, these shows sold out and further monies were raised for charity. In the following year, it was mooted again that we do three more dates, but after initial enthusiasm, it was decided that we would not improve on the previous shows, and we could quite possibly spoil the memories we had of the original shows. So, we decided to call it a day.

One last thought, about fourteen years ago, after Ray and I had both retired, and after having a few beers one night, we contemplated going back out again as a duo, calling ourselves 'Grumpy Old Men', I think it would have been a lot of fun, but I think our wives who had put up with all the years spent 'on the road' were not so keen. So we decided against it.

Back to the story...

GEORGE SCOTT PROMOTIONS…

AFTER I HAD left 'The Mavericks', and with three lifelong friends Peter Gunter, Derek Arch and Richard Barnwell we started earning a bit of extra cash promoting dances around the area in local town and village halls. As most of us were apprentices or not earning a lot, this helped improve our income. We called ourselves 'George Scott Promotions', as we thought it sounded 'trendy'.

In fact, the promoting was successful and we made headlines in the Daventry Weekly Express when we were stopped from hiring the Daventry Secondary Modern School, after being too successful. Newspaper cutting follows overleaf.

Teenagers 'Expelled' for their Enterprise

SCHOOL GOVERNORS AT DAVENTRY SECONDARY SCHOOL HAVE PUT A BAN ON A BIT OF TEENAGE ENTERPRISE — BECAUSE, THEY SAY, IT'S TOO ENTERPRISING.

And that means the end of visits of the teenagers rock 'n' roll stars to the town.

For the only suitable hall in Daventry for such dances is the Secondary School hall which has been hired out for four such dances.

Stars like Dickie Pride, Duffy Power, and Milton Ingram have been brought to the town by a "syndicate" consisting of 18-year-old Peter Gunter and three 19-year-olds Lawrence Wheeler, Derek Arch and Richard Barnwell.

Lawrence Wheeler and Richard Barnwell are both ex-pupils of the school.

The letter from the school managers refusing any further bookings of the school hall to the four gives no other reason than that the governors will not allow any further lettings for private gain.

The letter did state that the hall would not in future be let for functions on Saturday nights as it meant the caretaker having to clean up on Sunday mornings, but it is the ban on " private gain " which has put the young partnership out of business.

Ex-vocalist with the local Mavericks rock 'n' roll group — they are also " expelled " from the school — Lawrence Wheeler told the Weekly Express: "We did work in the hope of making a small profit—and were prepared to stand together in case of loss.

" And by attendances at the dances it was evident we were giving people of our own age what they wanted—an opportunity to meet the stars on the records they have bought or which they play on the juke-boxes."

Fellow Partner Derek Arch continued "Maybe the governors have never heard of any of these personalities we have brought to Daventry — maybe they are stars which do not exist in the governors' firmament—but they are very real people to teenagers.

"As to the question of working for private gain we are all apprentices and if we have managed to make a little extra pocket-money we have been glad of it—but it hasn't been done without hard work."

Concerning future plans for the dances Lawrence Wheeler said: "We were hoping to have even bigger stars next winter, and negotiations were under way for Mike Sarne—who took Come Outside into the hit-parade. Shane Fenton and the Fentones and Screamin' Lord Sutch and the Savages were also being considered.

"It doesn't seem so long ago that I was being told at that same school about the virtues of people who had amassed fortunes—because they were not afraid to do a bit for their own private gain.'"

All four boys take it as a slight against them and the teen-agers of Daventry, including ex-Secondary Modern school pupils.

Peter Gunter pointed out "We have run dances at Village halls in West Haddon, Heyford, Priors Marston, and the Co-op Hall, Northampton, a hall in Rugby and believe it or not a Church hall in Northampton, all without complaint."

"THAT'S THE REASON"

Chairman of the school's governors Ald. George Williams told the Weekly Express: "The objection to making private gain was the reason quoted by the governors for refusing the hall bookings.

"I do not want to make any comment except to say the decision was not reached without full thought.

"But, after all, this is a school hall first and foremost, and the school governors do not have to give reasons for their refusal."

Left: Newspaper clipping from Daventry Weekly Express in the early 1960s

THE START OF MY ENTERTAINMENT AGENCY

ONE DAY IN 1968, there was a knock on the door, and standing there was a group of lads from Daventry who were in a 4-piece music group called 'Trip to the Sun'. They said they knew of my musical connections and would I be interested in managing them for bookings. After a few days, I said that I would give it a try as their Manager/Agent. A few weeks later I was approached by a Rugby-based group 'Sam Spade and the Gravediggers' - an outrageous pop group, who asked me if I wanted to manage them also, to which I agreed so the agency started with my first two acts. I then went to my two local clubs, the Daventry Working Men's Club and the Daventry Social Club, who both gave me bookings at their clubs... so I was on my way.

I initially called the Agency 'Falcon Management' as we lived in Falconers Close, in Daventry, so it seemed to fit in well.

Because of the indecision of what was happening at the Daventry Weekly Express I had in the meantime moved to the Leamington Spa Courier newspaper. It was a daily 45-mile round trip. I worked there for about seven years, but in the meantime, the Agency got busier and busier, but I was still reluctant to do the Agency full time, as I did not like to be dependent on other folks' ability.

One day when reading the New Musical Express, I saw an advert for groups to work around Europe. It was just as the Beatles were getting recognised and the 'Mersey Sound' was becoming popular around the world. The agent, from Germany, was based in Manchester and was called the Paul Vonk Agency. He was holding auditions in London at a popular music pub called the 'Pied Bull' in Islington. He told me that a club owner in Belgium called Karl Storm was coming over to see the auditions to select groups to work in his 40-odd clubs throughout Europe and did my group 'Trip to the Sun', want to audition? They decided that they did, and along with seven other groups, on the day, auditioned.

After the audition, and following a discussion between Paul Vonk and Karl Storm, we were told that he wanted to book 'Trip to the Sun', to go out to Germany. The group had already decided that if they were offered work they would 'give it a go professionally'.

Their audition was successful and 'Trip to the Sun' were there and then offered a month's contract at the Taboo Club in Cologne for the month of October. The German agent then produced the contract and asked them to sign it, there and then. Unbelievably it was printed in German. I informed the club owner that they wanted to do the month's work, but they wanted to take the contract to be checked by the Musician's Union, to make sure that everything was in order. But he insisted that the contract had to be signed that day. I spoke to Paul Vonk, who you recall was our 'go between' agent, and he assured us that the contract was 'pretty standard', and there was nothing in there to worry about. So, the group signed the contract, and about a month later we set off for Cologne with great anticipation. The group were very excited as they saw it as their 'big break', and I was equally pleased because I felt that Falcon Management was going 'international'.

Unfortunately, the contract was nothing like 'standard', as when we got to the Taboo Club in Cologne, we were told that the group had to play seven nights a week from 8 pm to 4 am in the morning, three-quarters of an hour performing, and a quarter of an hour off. Which meant that they had to play six hours a night, every night for a month. But of course, we didn't find this out until we got there, so they were really left with no alternative. Bearing in mind in the UK they were usually expected to perform for a maximum of 2 hours a night, but usually around 90 minutes, this was really excessive. I even recall being called into the club Managers office after three nights to be told by the manager that the group were 'repeating' numbers! I pointed out that they were playing about 70 songs a night, and they just did not have that many, hence the repeats.

I know that this sounds idealistic, but I made a decision there and then to myself that I would never ask acts to do something that I wouldn't do myself, and I acted on this principle throughout the forty years I had my agency.

I came back after about four days as my agency work in the UK was building up, and 'Trip to the Sun' settled into the routine, and from all accounts enjoyed it. The month went well, and the promoter rang me to offer them the month of December in Egypt. At the end of October, when they returned from Germany, we had a meeting. If they took the Egypt booking they were going to be away from home over Christmas. They discussed it with the families, and as two of them had girlfriends they were put under pressure not to go, and the two single guys wanted to go, so there was a problem! They asked me what I would do in their position about the month in Egypt. I said to them that I understood them not wanting to be away in December, but when they look back later in life, all Christmases will blend into each other, whereas the Christmas in Egypt would always be memorable for them… they discussed it, there was a falling out, and they decided instead to split-up!!

The agency was getting more and more time-consuming, but I still continued to work in Leamington, until a couple of years later the matter was taken out of my hands somewhat. One Sunday afternoon I was playing football for my local pub side the Dun Cow against a team based in Rugby, and I broke my right leg. I was put into full-length leg plaster for four months, so was unable to drive to work at Leamington Spa, which enabled me to develop my agency full-time on the phone during the day from home. If I needed to go out to meetings, Jenny would drive me.

Luckily I had insurance, and was also paid my basic salary from work, so financially was no worse off. At the time there were not many agents about (not like now), there was one in Northampton, one in Coventry and a couple in Birmingham, so work was plentiful. After my leg was better, I returned to work at Leamington. During the four months I was off, the agency had more than trebled its turnover, and I have to say I was getting loads of work.

You probably won't believe the next part of the story, but about four months later after returning to work at Leamington, my friends from the Dun Cow rang again, and said they were short of a player again, would I turn out for them. They said they would put me on the 'wing', so I wouldn't be at much risk. So off to Brinklow near Rugby I went. After about ten minutes I found myself in the goalmouth and I scored. Unfortunately, the goalkeeper dived on my left leg and broke it. This meant another four months off work, fortunately – if that is the word – as it was the other leg, it meant I was paid out insurance again both from the football club and my work. If it had been the right leg, which I had broken previously, I would not have been insured.

Also at this time, I had a bit of a breakdown due to overwork. My doctor told me that I couldn't manage to work full-time and run the agency, or I would endanger myself, so after discussing it with Jenny, we agreed that I should give the agency a 'full-time go', or I could regret it later. The Courier Press were very good to me, and said that if it didn't work out, I could return to my job with them… fortunately it did.

As the agency began spreading nationally, I became involved with the Wheatsheaf Hotel and another agency called Stallion Entertainments, but I will cover that in another chapter about F&S Entertainments and the music shops.

I have, over the years, been fortunate to either book or promote most of the big groups from that period, to name just a few: Marty Wilde and The Wildcats, The Searchers, The Fortunes, Gerry & the Pacemakers, Jigsaw, Alvin Stardust, The Mojos, The Hollies, Black Sabbath, Millie Small, Gene Vincent, Tommy Bruce, The Who, Craig Douglas, Billy J Kramer and the Dakotas, The Move, ELO, The Bachelors, The Kinks and most of the groups from the 60s and 70s. There are some great stories to tell, and most of them were good to work with, and they left me with lots of memories.

One of my favourite stories was when I had Dave Berry who was enormously popular at the time with several hit records including his number one hit '*The Crying Game*'. He liked to come on stage with just a spotlight on him and use exaggerated hand movements. The entertainment secretary at a Luton club was told to make sure that Dave did not trip on the microphone wire as he moved towards the stage, so the secretary started winding the wire up around his arm and followed him about a yard behind, and then he tripped Dave Berry over, and then fell over him as well in an almighty heap. Both struggled to get up, and yet the 5ft tall entertainment secretary still managed to balance his cigarette in his mouth.

On another occasion, I had booked Tony Gerrard, a comedian who was in a wheelchair at a club in Birmingham, at the time I was on crutches after one of my football injuries. When we arrived, it turned out the entertainment manager at the club, was also in a wheelchair. He had no sense of humour and couldn't see the funny side of it. He looked at the two of us and said 'You are taking the p*** out of me, so you can f***off now!', and with that he had the doorman escort us off the premises! The truth is I don't think he had sold many tickets.

When I had Joe Brown at a club in Milton Keynes he requested on the night a private room so he could tune up his guitar. There were only two rooms at the club, one the Concert Room (which was full) and the other being the public bar. He insisted he needed that room emptied to tune his guitar, even though there was a darts match on that night, and the bar was quite full. But he was insistent and said he couldn't go on unless he could tune his guitar up first. So around 30 disgruntled darts players were made to leave and stand in the car park, while he tuned up his guitar in the 'games' room.

On another occasion, Alvin Stardust was appearing in Northampton, and he asked me during the evening if one of his band could purchase a chair he had taken a liking to in the changing room, which was also the club's committee room. I told him that he would have to have a word with the club. He never mentioned it again, and I forgot about it. Around 10am the following morning a police car arrived on the drive, and I was confronted by two policemen, who asked me if I knew anything about a missing chair. It turned out to be the 'Chairman's Chair' which was about 120 years old and very, very valuable. I rang Alvin's agent and told him about it and how valuable it was. He said it wasn't his fault, but he checked with the group, and it turned out, they claimed it got mixed up with their gear by 'accident' when they were packing up after the gig. It got returned later that week!

The police were called to another gig I had in Corby. I had 'The Bachelors', a very popular trio with lots of hit records to their credit. They were booked on an 'Irish-themed' show with comedian Jimmy Cricket. The word spread around that 'The Bachelors' were selling drugs at the gig, and the police arrived. What 'The Bachelors' were actually selling was health tablets and powders, which was a business they had set up separately. They must have been really good, as the boys looked the picture of health, and did a great show.

I have been quite surprised that there has not been any really big groups produced from the Northampton area. Ian Patterson of course, fronted 'Mott the Hoople', and odd musicians have done well, including John Shearer the drummer from Daventry, Freddie 'Fingers' Lee from Northampton, and Kevin Thompson from Long Buckby have all made a living from the music industry, along with one or two others. Whereas Rugby – just 11 miles away - produced some really fine groups in the 60s that had numerous hit records. There was 'The Fortunes' with *You've got your Troubles* and other hits, there was 'Jigsaw' who recorded *Sky High* and had hits on both sides of the Atlantic with that song. Also the group 'Pinkerton's Assorted Colours'. Other groups like 'Racing Snakes' were very popular, and James Morrison has, more recently, had several successful singles and albums.

I personally represented some great local middle-of-the-road groups, as well as 'Trip to the Sun' later there was also a superb all-round versatile group called 'Mixed Blessings' who always got rebooked wherever they appeared, also the Daventry group 'Penthouse' worked regularly around the area. I still on occasions bump into Mike Smith and Glyn Murray from 'Mixed Blessings' who are still performing solo or in groups, there are a lot of acts these days playing on the nursing home circuit, where they only have to play a one-hour session, and it is financially quite rewarding.

One other incident which gave the family much amusement, was when I had a phone call from the local Daventry Council in 2003. They informed me that they wanted someone to switch on the Christmas lights in early December. I thought 'how nice', with me being a local businessman for so many years, they wanted me to switch on the lights… they then asked if I could give them the telephone number for my daughter Alison, who was singing at the time in 'The Beautiful South' group, as they wanted to ask her to switch them on, which she did! The group as it was later split up, but she still sings with the 'splinter' group 'The South'.

Previous years, I had a couple of incidents which caused me concern. I was travelling back from Jersey in the Channel Islands to Birmingham airport after attending some of my shows, which I had done on quite a few occasions. The flight was usually around 50 minutes to Birmingham, but I realised after being up in the air for over an hour that the cabin staff were getting a bit concerned. One came over to me and asked if I would change my seat and sit next to the emergency exit. They said that the undercarriage wheels of the plane would not come down, and they were going to have to make an emergency landing if they could not release them.

After about another 30 minutes of circling around, there was a groaning as the wheels eventually came down, but the announcement over the intercom said that although the wheels had come down, they were not sure that they were locked safely, and wouldn't know until they landed. They did this very tentatively but luckily the wheels held and we came to an eventual stop on the outer perimeter of the airport. There was spontaneous applause both of relief and appreciation of the pilot's skill.

Two weeks later I was in Ireland setting up a tour with gigs in both Northern and Southern Ireland. I was staying at a hotel in Warren Point, where there had been eighteen people killed in fighting a couple of weeks before. It was a pleasant warm evening, and I strolled out of the hotel onto a patio-type area overlooking a large lake. The manager of the hotel came out to me urgently and suggested I came back into the hotel as he said there were probably fourteen rifles aimed at me from the woods across the lake, and I would be safer inside. He said he thought I looked like a policeman and could get shot at, so I returned quickly.

I started handling more cabaret acts and comedians, as well as the groups and booked most of the comedians from 'The Comedians' TV show. The outrageous Bernard Manning was one of my favourite people to deal with.

He had a remarkable memory, and once he had met someone and had a conversation with them, he could remember the smallest detail about them. He would quite often walk into a dressing room and say to a minor support act who perhaps hadn't worked with him for six months, how is your wife (and remember her name), and are you still interested in (his hobby), they would be amazed, he would follow this by asking 'can I use your gear mate, save setting mine up?', which of course they always said yes. He was a real character and a gentleman, not like his TV persona.

Bernard had a club in Manchester called the Embassy Club, and on Thursday, Friday and Saturday nights, he would not leave the club until 9 pm, after he had opened the show for the evening and welcomed members to the club. This meant that he would have to go on stage quite late if he was working in the Midlands. But he always arrived spot on time. He would get out of the car in his blue dress shirt and black dinner suit with his black patent shoes in his hand, have a quick word with the support acts and then go straight on stage. A real pro.

I started promoting touring shows also, and for seventeen years I had spring, autumn and Christmas shows on tour. I also had a touring pantomime every Christmas, with some really experienced professional entertainers.

The 'Wheeltappers and Shunters Club' TV show produced dozens of young comedians, mainly from the north of England, comedians like Colin Crompton, George Roper, Mike Reid, Jim Bowen, Charlie Williams, Lee Wilson, Jos White, Bernie Clifton. In fact between the two shows 'The Comedians' and 'Wheeltappers and Shunters Club' during the time it was on TV from 1971-1985, it engaged 160 different comedians, a large proportion of these worked partly through my agency during that period, and continued to right up until I retired in 2004.

Comedians, not requiring a lot of equipment meant that on occasions they and other acts would take two or even three bookings in a night, particularly Friday and Saturday nights. While lucrative for the artist, it did cause problems if the first show ran late. This particularly happened in the clubs in the Northeast, which was a 'graveyard' for comedians anyway.

In this part of the country in particular, artists would get booked on what was called 'nett deals', where they would be paid a guaranteed fee for, say 10 shows in 10 days. But the Northern Agents were crafty, and as Monday, Tuesday and Wednesday could be quiet with no work about, they would expect the act to do 'doubles' on Friday, Saturday and Sunday nights, to do their 10 shows in 10 nights. As you can imagine this caused all types of problems, with acts getting held up at the first booking and arriving late for the second booking, and that would cause problems for clubs and agents with timing and payment.

The worst case of 'doubling' I ever saw, was with the top American music group 'The Four Seasons'. It was a Saturday night, and a regular client had them 'doubling' in Derby and Coventry. The Derby venue was north of the city, and the Coventry venue was out of the city on the A45 main Birmingham road at the Matrix Hall. They were due at the Coventry booking to appear at 10.30pm, but hadn't arrived by 11.30pm. Eventually, they arrived and by the time they were set up and ready to go, it was after midnight. As the backing band eventually started playing, the lead singer, Frankie Valli came on and started to sing one of their big hits *'Sherry'*, only to be greeted by a shower of coins from the impatient audience. He promptly left the stage and absolutely refused to perform despite much pleading from the promoter. Eventually, to placate the audience who were getting very restless, the agent gave them all free tickets to the following week's show with Jerry Lee Lewis! Who says an agent's life is an easy one?!

Also, after-dinner speakers became very popular, especially sportsmen, on the 'after-dinner' circuit. The problem was sometimes keeping them sober before they spoke, which was generally around 10pm. Footballers were the worst, and yet cricketers like Ian Botham and David Gower, were professional through and through, as were most rugby players.

I had a call one day from the Cunard Shipping Line, one of the world's biggest cruise companies, who were arranging a rugby themed cruise. They had an English, Welsh and a Scottish player booked (sounds like a joke coming), but they wanted an Irish player also, and they particularly wanted Willie John McBride, who had led the British Lions to success. It was my first booking with Cunard and I wanted to impress, so I assured them that I could get him for them. So, I phoned the Irish Rugby Union, to try to make contact, and expected to be brushed off, but they immediately gave me his home number, which was completely unheard of. I phoned his home number and a timid, sweet-voiced lady answered and informed me that she was Mrs McBride, and Willie was out walking the dogs but would be back in about an hour. I gave her the details of the cruise etc., the fee and what was expected of him, which was a 45-minute speech on one night, and a 45-minute 'question and answer' session on another night. The rest of the cruise time was his own to relax and do whatever he wanted. Also, he was able to take his wife with him. An hour later I phoned back, a booming voice answered my call this time, and said *'Willie John here'*, I started to explain to him the details and requirements for the cruise, but he cut me short with *'don't worry explaining laddie, the missus is already ironing her frocks, just send the contract!'*

Jenny and I love cruising, but I heard a comment which made me smile the other day to describe people who 'do' cruising as: *'Newly Wed, Over Fed or Nearly Dead'*
A bit cruel that I thought!

Away from the ships, and back on land... On another occasion, I had Tommy Smith the ex-Liverpool footballer booked for a Sporting Dinner at St. Neots Conservative Club. Guest of honour was John Major, the local MP and the then Prime Minister. It was emphasised to me that it was going to be a very important evening, and it was strictly evening suit. So, when I sent the contract to Tommy, I put 'DJ for top table'. When I met him before the dinner, he was wearing the gaudiest dog-tooth jacket that I had ever seen. When I asked him why he wasn't wearing a dinner jacket as I had put DJ on the contract, he said that he thought that meant the disc jockey would be on the top table! Fortunately, he gave a football signed by the 'hard men of football' 'Chopper' Harris, Norman Hunter and himself to John Major for one of his charities, so he got away with it.

Another embarrassing moment I had was when I was travelling to Birmingham for a sporting dinner, and as I had had meetings in Manchester during the day, I was travelling down from the north. I had my dinner suit on the back seat. So, I pulled into a lay-by to get changed, which I often did. Unfortunately, as I removed my trousers to put the dinner suit trousers on, there was tapping at the window and there were two guys standing there. It turned out that I was in a doggin' area, and when I put the light on in my car to reach my suit, they took it as a signal that I was looking for some doggin' action! I swiftly left the scene!

On one memorable occasion, I had a 'Ladies Night' booked in Northampton. Top male striptease artist Rebel Red was booked for the night, and the show was due to start at 8pm. I was at home in my office, when I got a call around 8.20pm from Malcolm James who was compere for the evening telling me that Rebel Red hadn't arrived yet. So, I spoke to the entertainment secretary John at the club, who was not allowed into the concert room on 'Ladies Nights', and I told him to let the show start and when Rebel Red arrived to let Malcolm know. So, Malcolm opened the show, at about 8.45 with vocals and chat etc., then a really good-looking guy with a small case walked into the club, bought himself a half pint and sat down. John went over to him and introduced himself and asked him if he would like to be taken through to the dressing room. The guy agreed and John attempted to walk him the quickest way to the dressing room through the concert room where the show was on and the girls were screaming. He said to John, I don't want to walk through there. John thought 'fair enough, he doesn't want to be seen until he goes on stage'. So, he proceeded to walk him the long way round to the dressing room, and asked to get ready, and Malcolm would tell him the time he was due to go on, when he had finished his 'spot'.

John then continued the story to me: '*When Malcom had finished his opening spot, he came off the front of the stage and came through to me in the bar, I told him that Rebel Red had arrived and I had taken him through to the dressing room, he was now waiting for Malcolm to go and tell him what time he was required to perform. Malcolm left and went to sort him out with times etc. Within a minute Malcolm came back out into the bar where I was, and said 'are you taking the p***?, I asked 'why?', so Malcolm had me follow him back to the dressing room. When we entered the guy was there all dressed up ready to perform... in a full deep sea diving suit. I couldn't believe it, and asked 'you are Rebel Red the stripper, aren't you?' to which* *the gent replied 'No, I am Tony James and I come here to give a deep sea diving demonstration!'.* It turns out that the Aqua Club held their monthly meetings at the club, and it had been cancelled because of the ladies' show, and they had failed to tell Tony James! I am so glad he never went out on stage in his full rubber suit and oxygen cylinders on his back, he would have got ravaged! Fortunately Rebel Red did arrive later, so it worked out OK in the end.

I would on occasion get asked for unusual types of entertainment. A very good customer of mine, who always booked his company functions through me, so when he asked for anything, I would, of course, do my utmost to supply it.

One day he phoned and said he had two very good friends who wanted to get their own back on another friend and customer (we can call him Jim) of theirs who was a practical joker and had pulled many practical jokes on them. They had booked individual rooms in a hotel in anticipation of having a guy's night out before returning later. They wanted me to arrange a young lady who would be let into Jim's room while they were out. They wanted her to strip to her underwear and get into the bath for when he arrived back at the hotel after the night out. The friends would ring the room, where the young lady was, and she would get into the bath, start running the water, and lay prostrate, scantily clad, and (horror!) throw theatrical blood all over herself and up the mirror etc. in the room. This was intended to give the guy a shock and to get their own back for previous practical jokes he had played on them over the years.

Unfortunately, and I will use the young lady's words as she told me, this happened: *'I was in his room waiting for the signal of his arrival, which I got, so I got myself ready in the bath with fake blood all over me and the bathroom walls. He came into the bedroom, but he must have dropped onto the bed and fell asleep. His friends were outside the door expecting their friend to scream out, at least. After about five minutes they realised that he must have fallen asleep, so they went to their rooms and phoned him in his room. He awoke from an alcohol-fuelled sleep to be told that they were the night porters, and it had been reported that there was a leak in his bathroom, could he please check it? By then I was laid prostrate in the bath with theatrical blood all over me, and he entered the bathroom, looked at me in semi-darkness in confusion, and thought I was his girlfriend and asked me what I was doing there? He then noticed that I was not his girlfriend and also noticed the blood everywhere. He grabbed his chest and started moaning and groaning. I realised that it was all going wrong and got out of the bath and moved towards him as I thought he was having a heart attack. This made him worse and as I was going towards him with fake blood dripping off me everywhere, he screamed out for me to keep away, and I thought he was going to have a heart attack and he dropped onto his bed groaning. Then his two mates came through the door and thought it hilarious. Unfortunately, their friend Jim did not find it at all funny and swore they would never get any work from him again!'...*

Luckily my friend the booker thought it was hilarious and tipped the young lady an extra £50.00.

This seems a good place and time to mention a conversation I had many years ago with Jenny, when she said to me, 'why do you book acts like that?', and I explained… if a regular client who spends thousands of pounds with me during the year, wants something different, if you don't supply it to them, someone else will. That is the business I am in.

There are so many stories to tell, but a question I get asked quite often is, have I turned an act down that has gone on to be successful? We have all heard the story of the record company who turned the Beatles down... Well, I missed out on a couple of opportunities, although the first one was not my fault.

In 1974, I had a group, a 6-piece from Leicester, they were called 'Noah's Ark'. They had two front vocalists who were great and also wrote their own songs. So, I contacted Mervyn 'Muff' Winwood, who I mentioned earlier from when I lived in Birmingham, who played in 'The Spencer Davis Group', and 'Traffic', and was the brother of Stevie Winwood. When 'Muff' left 'Traffic', he went to Island Records as a Record Producer. I sent him a cassette of the group, hoping he might get around to listening to it sometime.

Amazingly he came back to me the very next day and requested to know where the band were next playing, as he thought they were brilliant and wanted to see them performing live. He intimated that if they were as good as they sounded he would be interested in recording them.

They were due to perform at a club in Northampton the following Friday night, so he drove up from London to watch them. After the show, he informed me that he had a song that he wanted recording, but he only wanted the front two vocalists from the group, not the four musicians who backed them. He said that the backing musicians looked miserable and that the drummer looked like he had a big mortgage and three children. Which was quite ironic, as the drummer was the only single guy in the group. He also went later into politics in life and became an MP and was knighted for his services and became Sir Greg Knight.

But 'Muff' said he could get better musicians in London to do the backing on the record. I told the group this, but the initial reaction was: 'No, we are a group and he either takes us as a group, or not at all'. So, he intimated they might regret it, but he returned to London. A couple of weeks later I had a call from 'Noah's Ark' to say that they had changed their mind - that the two vocalists would do the recording, and if successful they could always bring the other members of the group in later.

When I informed 'Muff' of this, he just said no, he had another act to do it. Subsequently the chosen duo 'Sparks' had an enormous hit with *'This Town Ain't Big Enough for Both of Us'*, which reached Number 2 in the charts and won 'Muff' the award of 'Record of the Year 1974'. So 'Noah's Ark's chance of stardom had passed.

Another instance was when my niece Jayne phoned me to say she was waitressing at a restaurant in Birmingham, and there was 'a man with a lovely voice' who sang in the restaurant. She asked if she could bring him over to my office for me to meet him, which she did. He brought a cassette of his songs with him. He had a superb semi-classical voice. After listening to his perfect voice, I said to him, that there was no doubt he would always work, but I said that he would never make a living from it... Eighteen months later he was number 1 all around the world with a female vocalist as 'Renee and Renato' and their enormous hit *'Save Your Love'* which was a worldwide hit. Several years later I booked Renato for a cabaret night at a venue in Luton, and we had a good laugh about it as he drove off in his Bentley!

One act I would have loved to manage was 'Canned Rock' they were a three-piece group based around the Luton area and were an unbelievably talented trio. At the time I was managing a comedian called Billy Jay, and he got through to the finals of 'Pub Entertainer of the Year', which was going out live on ITV. I knew 'Canned Rock' well, as they had done quite a lot of work for me. That evening they were superb, they played Tchaikovsky's *'1812 Overture'*, which from a trio of musicians was show-stopping. Everyone thought they should have won it but during an advert break in the show I picked up the feeling that the winners had already been decided and subsequently, a country and western group won it. The whole thing had a bad smell about it.

Don Maxwell, the leader of 'Canned Rock' and I found solace in drink that night - Don because he felt he had been fiddled out of winning, and me because Billy Jay changed his act to 'blue material' during his act, and as it was a live transmission, they cut his act short and told him he would never work TV again! During our sorrowful drinking session afterwards with Don, I offered to suspend operations of my agency for a year, just to promote 'Canned Rock', I was that certain about their chances of success. But Don said he wanted to retain management himself. It was a pity, and I occasionally still see him working around the pubs, where we have a beer and talk about what might have been.

One of the other questions I get asked is if there is anything I particularly don't like about the business. Well, I have never liked 'miming' or 'lip-syncing' as it is now called. It is surprising how many acts used to mime, even on so-called 'live' shows. I remember some groups didn't even bother to plug their instruments in to look as if they were playing. Bearing in mind my start with the 'Fabulous Satellites', it is a bit of a cheek of me!

Also, another thing that annoyed me, was 'riders' on contracts, this was particularly bad in the 60s/70s. A 'rider' is anything an act demands on their contract, over and above the date, fee and performing times etc. to be supplied in the dressing room on the night of their booking. Depending on the stature of the act, sometimes it might be a bottle of whisky or brandy, or it could be bottles of wine, beers or flowers. One very famous female diva would insist that the hallway and ceiling from her dressing room to the stage had to be painted white, or she wouldn't leave her dressing room. A top recording group famously insisted that a dish of M&Ms was left in the dressing room, with the brown ones taken out. Their logic in this was that if the 'rider' was adhered to, it meant that the contract had been read thoroughly.

Coming up to present times. I retired and sold the 'Lawrence Wheeler Agency' in 2004 to an artist who worked for me and knew most of my venues. His name is James Honour (good name for an agent!), and he still operates it under the name 'Lawrence Wheeler Agency'. I'm pleased to say the agency has just passed its 60th Anniversary.

I still go out on occasion to see the odd show, but the days of driving up and down motorways are long gone now. A couple of things that weren't about when I was travelling so much, and which I regret not having, were sat-navs and mobile phones. To be able to keep in touch with the office or home by mobile phone would have been a dream, and also when I think about the nights I have been driving around cities in the dark looking for clubs or theatres I certainly could have done with a sat-nav.

But I have been very lucky, and the entertainment business has been superb for me. It has given me forty years I could never forget.

Below: Programme from FA Youth Cup
Birmingham City v. Northampton Town 1959

Above: Regular Daventry Town FC
Supporters. Left to right: myself,
Mike Tebbitt and Jim Henderson

Above: Touring with Captain Hawkins
team in Australia in the early 1980s.
I am on back row furthest left.

Above: Showing my support for Daventry Town during
the early 2000s

Above: Playing for Wellingborough
Rugby team in 1983, I am on back
row furthest right

Above: George Scott Promotions. The picture shows me with Peter Gunter on left, and Derek Arch on right, unfortunately Richard Barnwell was not available that night. Circa 1961/62

Above: 'Trip to the Sun' my first ever signing with Lawrence Wheeler Agency

Above: Alvin Stardust

THE BEAUTIFUL SOUTH

Above: Our daughter, Alison in
'The Beautiful South'

Above: Bernard Manning

Above: Dave Berry
performing back in the day

Above: Recording artists and pop stars who
worked for me, left to right: Joe Brown, Marty
Wilde, Billy Fury and Mark Winter

Above: Willie John McBride

Above: Show Posters

"NOAHS ARK"

Above: The group 'Noah's Ark'.
Greg Knight is standing on the right

Above: Sir Greg Knight

Above two photos: Mixed Blessings

Above: Joe Brown...
keeping in tune!

Above: Tommy Smith

Above: Renee and Renato

Above: Canned Rock

THE WHEATSHEAF HOTEL
& NURSING HOME

I SEEM TO recall that it was a Sunday afternoon in around 1980 that I had a phone call from a friend and local landlord at the Dun Cow pub in Brook Street, John Birch. The pub had been my 'local' for many years, and I was a regular and had gotten very friendly with John and the great atmosphere he encouraged… though at times over the coming years there would have been occasions that I had wished that I had not been at home that Sunday afternoon to take his call.

John had phoned me to tell me that the Wheatsheaf Hotel at the top of Sheaf Street was becoming available, as the widowed lady owner Mrs Cherry was retiring. To be truthful she was not the easiest lady to get along with and was known to 'shoo away' anyone she did not like who came into the Wheatsheaf bar, and chase them out with a broom. John told me that, along with Resh Singh* who had the very successful Swiss Cottage Hotel** at the top of Sheaf Street they were considering putting in a bid to purchase the Wheatsheaf Hotel, and they were looking for a third partner to go into the venture sharing it equally, and was I interested? Although I didn't know too much about Resh then, I told them I would give it some thought. I later agreed to join them as an equal partner each holding 30%, and we put the remaining 10% on hold for the time being.

On reflection, it was not a good move for me. John and Resh wanted to make it a top-class 5-star hotel and a restaurant like the 'Butcher's Arms' at Priors Hardwick was at the time. We had to borrow from the bank to cover the high cost of trying to change the hotel into a 5-star. John took over as paid Manager of the 'Wheatsheaf Hotel', while Resh ran his 'Swiss Cottage' and I looked after my entertainment business. There were various reasons that it did not work out, but after eighteen months John wanted to step down and return to the Dun Cow pub, which in the meantime had lost a lot of customers, as John had not been there.

We needed a third partner, and as we were in debt it was difficult to interest anyone. Eventually, we were joined at the Wheatsheaf Hotel by Resh's sister Goodie Kaur, who had run the Elizabethan Restaurant (now known as Windsor Lodge) in New Street successfully for many years. Goodie was an excellent business partner and also a first-class chef, so she was ideal for the Wheatsheaf. With just 17 bedrooms the hotel could not generate enough business to cover costs, and it was not as successful as we had hoped. We were very fortunate that a local businessman Darryl 'Chalky' White who had a car sales and maintenance business in Daventry took on the spare 10% which helped us out financially and saved us from going out of business.

Though not a great success financially, there are so many stories to tell about the hotel, as every week there seemed to be problems. One I recall was when a touring cricket team stayed at the hotel for seven nights while playing at Midlands-based cricket clubs. The morning after their first night at the hotel, I was greeted by Dennis our resident caretaker and night watchman and told that one of them had stolen two of the valuable original paintings from the bar wall. This stood out particularly as in those days smoking was still allowed inside and there were two clear blank areas on the wall where the paintings had been.

Dennis tipped us off as to who had stolen them, and the cleaner, when cleaning the hotel bedroom 'accidentally' knocked the resident's case open, and there they were, in fact, there were three items he had stolen. The touring team were playing a local village side on that day. We advised the Daventry police about the thefts, and when the team returned from playing, they were greeted by the Daventry police who had very great pleasure in arresting the guilty party… Oh, I omitted to mention, the visitors were a touring police cricket team! So, you can imagine the uproar this caused.

Also, we would often have parties of 'ghost hunters' stay at the hotel, as the hotel was considered by many as haunted, particularly during the first weekend in June. Folk would sit up all night hoping to witness a visit from the resident ghost.

I remember when we first moved into the hotel, we just kept the old downstairs bar open while we worked on the alterations to the hotel. We would take it in turns to run the bar, and on this one Sunday evening I was working an old friend Pete Gunter had called in during the evening for a drink wearing his red Wales football shirt. He said he was going down to the Dun Cow for a drink and would call back later. It was after closing time, and I was cashing up on my own when I raised my head and saw who I thought was Pete standing in the doorway. I said 'I won't be a minute', but there was no reply. I then thought that the person I had seen was wearing a helmet and red tunic. I called out 'Is that you, Pete?' There was still no reply, so I went to the doorway he had been standing in, and there was no one there! I locked up and shot out as quickly as I could! There are so many ghost stories to tell. In the meantime we got the hotel running, but it was always a struggle...

One day when chatting in the bar, a customer mentioned that there was a shortage of residential and nursing home beds in the South Northants. Around 1989/90, we approached the local Northampton Health Authority who said that they would be very happy to accommodate local residents at the newly refurbished Wheatsheaf Court Nursing Home, previously the Wheatsheaf Hotel. Because the bedrooms were big, and because we did not need a room for a bar etc., we were able to change the Hotel into a 53-bed Nursing Home. This immediately became successful, Resh and Goodie then asked me if I would take over as Manager and run the nursing home, and Goodie took over cooking and running the kitchen.

Managing the nursing home was a unique experience for me. I found that during most of the day I was dealing with entertainment artists, who to them a 'wrongly' coloured dressing room was a major catastrophe... and then perhaps a nursing home resident who was maybe poorly, elderly and had no visitors. It was a different world and gave me a different value of what is good in life, and I struck up some wonderful friendships with the residents.

Around the mid/late 1990s, Resh was not well, and Goodie wanted to return to running her own café/restaurant, which she did in Banbury and later Rugby. My agency was extra busy so around the late 1990s we decided to sell the nursing home business.

A pharmacist who had a chemist shop at the Bull Ring in Birmingham wanted to purchase a nursing home. After viewing the Wheatsheaf, he made us an offer we couldn't - and didn't want to - refuse. Obviously, he knew how to run a successful business, as I hear at the last count he now has at least thirteen nursing homes around the UK, mostly in the Midlands.

So after having spent the previous twenty years at first a hotel and then a nursing home, I must admit I was very relieved to be out of it and be able to continue in the entertainment business which had been successful, and my life.

*Resh Singh's son is none other than popular local café owner Ricky Singh, who can be found most days at the busy Kitchen café in Bowen Square.

**The Swiss Cottage Hotel was located opposite the Wheafsheaf Hotel at the top of Sheaf Street. My wife Jenny used to serve behind the bar at the Wheatsheaf Hotel on Friday nights, then go across to the Swiss Cottage afterwards to serve in the night club (she will tell you that she worked for 12 years behind the bar at the Wheatsheaf Hotel and Swiss Cottage, without any pay!).

In 1985, we came back from holiday and our daughter Lisa met us at the airport and said she had 'some good news and some bad news', Jenny asked her what was that, she replied 'the good news is that you do not have to work at the Swiss Cottage anymore, the bad news is that it burnt down!'... which was a slight exaggeration.

The Swiss Cottage was set fire to by young folk (around 12 years of age and early teens) on a Sunday afternoon. Fortunately, they were caught later in the afternoon by the police. Otherwise they might have thought it was a deliberate fire started by us! It wasn't a big fire and it certainly never burnt down. It did reopen again later.

MY NIGHT CLUB SCENE

IT WAS IN the 1980s, at around the same time I had got involved with the Wheatsheaf Hotel, that I was chatting one day with my very good lifelong friend Richard Stockil, and he informed me that he had the opportunity to have the former old Methodist church (now Chasers) as a pub and night club in New Street, Daventry and was I interested in getting involved with him?

Initially, there were going to be four partners in the venture, along with Richard and I - the others being Errol Baxter who was a popular young man about town at the time and Kevin Wright who had tried on his own to get a club 'running'. The initial name for the club was Rosie O'Grady's, then later on, Madisons.

It was quite financially challenging early on, as most businesses are, and Kevin left to go elsewhere. Errol had the chance of being the 'Landlord' of the popular Beachcomber pub on Bowen Square in Daventry, and you really couldn't stand in his way. After about 18 months, I just could not cope with involvement with the pub/night club, hotel and my other businesses, so after agreeing with Richard, I stepped away. Glad to say though we are still the best of friends.

Richard owned/managed the business for the next thirty years or so, and it had several different names during that time, including 'Jesson's Well', 'Rainbows' and 'Freddies'. The pub/club currently operates under the name of 'Chasers'. It is without doubt one of the most popular venues in town.

MUSIC, INSTRUMENTS, VIDEO SHOPS AND FLATS

IN THE EARLY 1980s my life was pretty busy with the established entertainment agency and the Wheatsheaf taking up a lot of time. I was also managing a five-piece group from Rugby called 'Leo' who were a very popular middle-of-the-road group. Their base player was a musician I knew named Vince Dunne, as well as performing in the group he also had a music shop at 4 Sheaf Street, Daventry, where he sold keyboards, guitars and other instruments. Vince also had a small part-time entertainment agency himself which he operated. He suggested that we amalgamate our agencies and the music shop as one business partnership. He said it would enable him to take care of the shop and be part of the new joint agency and I could carry on with my part of the agency and also the Wheatsheaf Hotel and Rosie O'Grady's nightclub in New Street.

So we merged the businesses and named the new agency 'F&S Entertainments'. After about six months Vince had seen a shop property in Henry Street, Rugby. He thought we could make a great success of it, as there were not any similar music shops in Rugby at the time. Also - and this is where we slipped up - there were four flats above the shop. After discussing this we thought we could 'let' them out as furnished flats, but we decided that we would only have female residents, as we thought that they would take greater care of the properties! Boy, were we wrong!

Unfortunately, this was one big mistake. We suddenly found out that these girls were having parties every Friday and Saturday night, with lots of boys and girlfriends there. Vince seemed to get a call most weekends from the police, complaining about the noise and disruption coming from above the music shop in Rugby.

On the plus side, we had also started the first video clubs in Daventry and

Rugby, and this was proving very successful. I recall that we made a special 'opening offer' where we offered to rent out 100 videos for £100. This proved very popular, but we suddenly realised we hadn't got enough videos initially to cover the hiring out.

A little story that always brings a smile is when my wife Jenny was covering the Daventry shop one Saturday morning when our regular assistant had rung in sick. A lady customer called in and said that she was looking after her grandchildren for the weekend, and she would like a video that she could let them play. She asked Jenny if she could recommend any particular video tapes? Jenny asked her if the child had any preferences and was told that he likes 'space travel' stories and films, so they looked down the list of videos available and saw one called 'Wham, Bam, Thank You Spaceman'. She asked Jenny if she knew what it was like, but she said that she had never watched it.

The Grandmother said she would take it, and she was sure that they would enjoy it… on the following Monday, Jenny was again covering the shop as the regular assistant was still unwell. The Grandmother walked in to return the video. She was not a happy lady. You have probably guessed it by now, but it was a rather sexy video! Jenny fully apologised and refunded the Grandmother the hire fee. As the Grandmother walked out, she turned around and commented with a twinkle in her eye: 'The children didn't like it, but my husband and I did!'

Returning to the shops, it just was not working out between Vince and I, so we decided to return to how we were before merging. I stepped away from the shops, and Vince from the agency, so we were able to pick up where we had been eighteen months previously. In fact, after that Vince started working for me again in a trio he had started. Vince carried on with the shops, and I rebuilt the agency which had suffered when there were the two of us and the problems which had arisen. I was still involved with the Wheatsheaf Hotel, and with the Rosie O'Grady's Night Club for a while. Though after a discussion with Richard, I stepped down from the club and concentrated on the agency, which was busy, busy, and the Wheatsheaf, which was still a hotel at the time.

Below: The Wheatsheaf Hotel official 'Opening' after restoration in 1982

Above: King Charles Ist
who stayed at the hotel prior to the
'Battle of Naseby' in June, 1645

Above: The certificate for the re-opening given
to us by the Mayor.

Above: The Wheatsheaf Hotel in the early 1950s

Above: The Wheatsheaf Hotel as it was before we took over ownership in the early 1980s.
As you can see it required a lot of work to be done on it.

Above: The Wheatsheaf Hotel building in 2023

Above: Resh and his sister, Goodie, in the early 1980s

Left: I just loved taking care of the nursing home residents

Above: Wheatsheaf Court Nursing Home outing to Bognor Regis for a four-day break. The residents loved it, and the staff did too.

Below: Ravi Patel bought the Wheatsheaf Court Nursing Home from us

Above two photos: Madisons Night Club

Above left: Resh and Barry McGuigan MBE (World featherweight boxing champion (1985-86)

Above right: Richard with the famous Sir Geoff Hurst, England's hat-trick scoring hero in the1966 World Cup. Both were guests on different 'Sporting Dinners' at the club

Left: The property when it was a Methodist Church

Left: The building in 2023, now called Chasers Bar & Lounge

Left: 4 Sheaf Street, Daventry pictured in 2023 – this was the site of our Daventry music shop

Left: The site of our Rugby music shop and flats pictured in 2023

Above: Thank you to all for your continued help with the
'Thank you Daventry . . . for the Memories' page
Left to right: Jason Rodhouse, William Philpott, Myself,
Barbara Crockford, David Knight and Andy (Catshed)

Left: True friends are some of the most
treasured things
Left to right: Peter Payne, myself, Peter Gunter,
Clive Pittaway and Richard Stockil

THANK YOU DAVENTRY
. . . FOR THE MEMORIES

I regard myself as having had a very lucky life, and as my wife and I both celebrate our 80th birthdays in relatively good health, I hope that we will continue to do so.

I'd like to thank all the funny, kind, interesting and, frankly, extraordinary people I have met over the decades, to thank my wife and daughters for their relentless support, and Nina and Mike for their enlightening and heartwarming contributions.

I genuinely believe that Daventry has a bright and exciting future ahead as more new houses and businesses are attracted to this relatively quiet corner of beautiful Northamptonshire. Above all, I'd like thank Daventry for all its charms and for the opportunities that have been afforded to me in this delightful market town. Thank you Daventry . . . for the memories!

GROWING UP IN DAVENTRY

Nina Cashmore Life Article

ALTHOUGH NOT ACTUALLY born in Daventry I have lived here since I was six weeks of age, so I was almost born and bred here, but not quite. I grew up on Ashby Road, opposite the school, which incidentally wasn't there when my parents had the house built in 1949. In those days there were just views over the beautiful countryside and cows looking over the back garden fence. My dad Gordon Turner worked as an engineer at the BBC radio station on Borough Hill and my mum Ivy stayed at home to look after me and my older siblings Sue, Steve and Mark. In the 1960s and early 1970s there wasn't much housing beyond Daneholme Park, no Ashby Fields, Middlemore, Micklewell or Monksmoor and Lang Farm was exactly that, a farm, not a housing estate!

Some of my earliest memories are of shopping in town with mum, which we seemed to do almost every day. Most shops specialised and we knew exactly where to go for each particular thing we needed. Baxters, Higgs, Colletts, Hillmans, Jeggos, Masons and the Co-Op Drapery were some I remember, but my favourite was England's sweet shop. All those glass bottles of heavenly delights! Milk Bottles, Butterscotch Humbugs, always wrapped up in a twist of paper. But we only went there once a week. We used to have Corona Cherryade pop delivered to the house occasionally. And milk in glass bottles, (which were sent back for recycling). The birds used to peck the foil tops off now and then. The tops that survived pecking were washed, collected and given to a charity.

Occasionally a passing tramp would knock on our door and ask for a drop of water for his billy can. Mum would also give him some sandwiches too. She was always kind to people and cooked dinner every day for our elderly next door neighbour in his latter years. Women would often talk over the fence to their neighbours back then, as most were at home and people didn't put up high fences. I think communities were more closely knit as a result.

As we lived right opposite the school, I attended Falconers Hill Infants and Juniors and Ashby Road Secondary Schools. Years 1 and 2 of Secondary were at the old Grammar School on North Street, so that was a bit further afield, and I still used to come back home for lunch! Some of my favourite teachers were Mrs Sturgess, Miss Boyes, Mr Austin, Mr Dent, Miss Bradbury and Mr Everett. I wasn't a studious child and spent most of my time in lessons staring out of the windows at the fields and wishing I were there instead.

Mum and dad were very involved with the Daventry Christian Assembly on the Market Square and I attended services there on Sunday mornings and evenings and Sunday School in the afternoon. We also had midweek meetings at our house on Tuesday and Wednesday evenings. I never resented the time spent there as we always had a lot of fun and had regular outings to meet up with young people from other churches. My faith is very important to me and has helped me through difficult times in my life.

I loved going up the road to Daneholme Park with my brother when I was young. There were iron railings around the park in those days, and kissing gates. We'd climb trees and go onto the old railway line, which didn't have a path on it at the time. The line had closed just before I was born, but some of the sleepers and track were still in place. Another favourite place to play was the rubbish dump further down Ashby Road, where Shackleton Drive is now. The gates were often open and we would go in and jump up and down on old mattresses and see if we could find anything interesting.

We visited the rec fairly often too and I liked the big slide and the see saw. The Witches Hat was terrifying and the roundabout made me feel sick. When I was very small mum used to pick me up and plonk me in the cab of the old train and I just remember the smell of wee and worse, but when I got older I'd venture further around the old engine and actually last year I was commissioned to paint a picture of it, which helped me to understand it a bit better.

My parents grew loads of vegetables in the large back garden and I spent a lot of time out there helping with that and I still love gardening and the outdoors now. We used to get together with the neighbours John and Doreen Lodge and their family on November 5th and have a huge bonfire with a 'Guy' on the top and boxes of Jumping Jacks, Catherine Wheels, Bangers and Sparklers. Slightly dangerous, but fun!

With my pocket money I'd go round to the shop on the Headlands and often buy a Curly Wurly or an Icebreaker, and a book for about 15p. I grew up without tv, so I read a lot, especially books about ponies. Our parents always encouraged us to be creative and praised us when we did something well. My older brother Steve Turner went on to become a very successful writer and author. I also spent a great deal of time drawing and dad used to get huge rolls of lining paper for me to draw landscapes and horses on. I was mad about all things equine and went to work at Major Cheyne's hunting stables in Badby when I left school, instead of going to art college, which my art teacher Mr Dent had advised me to do.

Another place I really loved going to was the outdoor swimming pool. What fun we had there! Many happy evenings and Saturdays, come rain or shine. You could take a picnic and stay all day, for about four pence. I liked the big Dairy toffees, Mo Jos and Fruit Salad sweets, Snaps and tomato soup in a polystyrene cup that they sold in the shop there. (Fortunately I'm a much healthier eater now!) I used to love queuing up outside on a hot day and seeing the blue water through the glass doors. It always looked so inviting. Oh, and the chocolate machine just inside the door, ha ha! My sweet tooth. We were outside most of the time in those days and used to ride our bikes everywhere, even out to quite far flung villages. Once, when riding our bikes down on The Willows I swapped with my friend who had a 'Tomahawk' and I couldn't steer it properly. I went over the handlebars and hit my head on the tarmac, suffering mild concussion. (That probably explains a lot!) The roads were much quieter then and generally our parents didn't worry about our safety so much. We had a lot of freedom.

In my teens, me and my friend Abigail would dress up in our safety pins and ripped shirts and wander around the town shouting at the Punks from Southbrook school. Well, my friend did most of the shouting as I was the quiet one. We would try to buy records we had heard on the John Peel radio show from Creighton's music shop, (now First Light Photographic), but they never sold the obscure ones we liked. We had to go to Vickys in Rugby for those. Together we produced a couple of issues of a fanzine and sold them at school. In it we wrote about our favourite bands, reviewed new records and also included some pics of our friends, enemies and musicians. It was quite cheeky really and I don't think the teachers approved. We weren't the best behaved pupils and just wanted to have a laugh instead of concentrating on our studies. As a result, we didn't leave with a huge stack of GCE's. But we found our way eventually, and Abigail is now a very accomplished seamstress, clothing the rich and famous and designing and making her own fashion line.

There wasn't an awful lot going on in Daventry in the 1970s and 80s and we had to make our own entertainment, which was probably no bad thing. We learnt to use our imaginations and be creative. There was also not much to spend our money on, so we saved. Not so much to eat either, so we starved. (Joking! But there really wasn't. No Maccy D's etc…)

I left school in 1980 and went to work with horses, which had always been my dream. Later in life I worked at a factory on London Road called Kohen Windsor, packing car parts for Fords. Many Daventry people did time there at some point in their lives and I was sentenced to 10 years. Finally, I was released to have my first child Jasper. Tabi came along 5 years later. By this time, I was married to Mike Cashmore who came from the other side of town and our rival school Southbrook. Our first house was in Balliol Road on the Stefen Hill estate. Housing estates had been springing up all around Daventry over the years and we eventually found ourselves living on Lang Farm, which had been green fields way beyond our town when we were young.

For most of my life I have drawn, but I didn't start painting until I was about forty. Soon after that I won a Rotary Club art competition with my 'Daventry' painting, and it was hung in Danetre Hospital and since then I have been busy with commissions and painting has become more of a full-time thing for me. For a few years now, I've worked from a small studio/gallery at Old Dairy Farm Craft Centre and Café, near Weedon, where I also sell prints and eat cake.

I like painting pictures of places I'm familiar with and have done several of the town. What I'd really like is for Daventry to have a big injection of colour to make it look like it does in my pictures. Imagine if Daventry looked like Notting Hill, only better? Maybe it could, with a bit of imagination and few pots of paint! I love colour and the way it just brightens everything up and makes you feel happy.

Although I sometimes think I would like to live somewhere else, Daventry is in my blood and I would find it hard to leave.

Nina Cashmore, local artist, kindly donated her artwork within this book for free so that the full cover price could go to local charities. If you'd like to purchase copies of her paintings, please visit her Facebook page for contact information or email her via ninacashmore@gmail.com.

Holy Cross

MY HOME TOWN

Mike Tebbitt Life Article

I HAVEN'T BEEN far in my life! Daventry to Welton and back, a distance of about two miles in little short of four-score years. Yet my earliest memories are of bomb-blitzed Coventry, not my small Northamptonshire home town.

At the age of three in 1947 my parents drove me round Coventry in the family Standard 10 car to look at the war-ravaged city whose munitions factories had attracted so much attention from German bombers. Every other building seemed to be in ruin, not to mention the original cathedral. Those visions still remain with me as do recollections of backing my first 'winner' at Towcester racecourse when aged just five. The horse was Blue John, the jockey Dave Dick, and I have been hooked on racing ever since.

About the same time I attended a birthday party at Drayton House, the home of Northamptonshire and England cricket captain Freddie Brown who was 'down under' at the time leading his country against Australia in the 'Ashes' series.

One of his sons, like me, must have been about five then and his iced birthday cake complete with stumps, bat and ball. This would have been made by his Mother's family business, Huntley and Palmers Biscuits.

I still have a treasured signed copy of Brown's memoirs, 'Cricket Musketeer' published in 1954.

But what of my home town you may ask? In my childhood the population of Daventry was under 6,000, not much more than the present population of Long Buckby. Daventry now has more than 30,000 residents but the small town historical background still prevails.

The Wheatsheaf, Saracen's Head, Dun Cow and Peacock (now the Halifax Building Society) are reminders of the town's Coaching Inn past on the route from London to Birmingham and beyond. To this day the town centre is made up of a triangle of streets comprising High Street, Sheaf Street and New Street.

Rapid post-war expansion came from the need to house British Timken workers from Birmingham (Braunston Road estate), Ford Motor Company employees from Essex (Southbrook estate) and the Birmingham overspill (Grange estate). More recently have come the three 'Ms', Middlemore, Monksmoor and Micklewell followed by Staverton Lodge close to the new bypass.

That bypass was meant to have been a dual carriageway but downgraded to single line traffic because of problems with underground streams on nearby Fox Hill. Have you noticed that dips are appearing in the road surface itself in recent years? Daventry itself is the 'nearly' town. The Grand Union canal just missed us, so to did the main railway lines out of London and the Roman A5 road as well as the M1 Motorway itself. Mad-cap schemes to provide Daventry with a modern canal arm and a pod-car transport system have thankfully failed to see the light of day.

Daventry's biggest 'near miss' though came in 1645 when the town narrowly escaped giving its name to the second most important battle in English history. The battle of Naseby (English Civil War} ranks second only to the Battle of Hastings. Had King Charles' army remained on Borough Hill and not attempted to reach Leicester, then the battle of Daventry would have become engraved in the minds of all school children.

Changes though have been numerous, some for the better and some for the worse. As a child living in the white bungalow opposite the main entrance to Danetre Hospital. I could walk out of the back garden and into open fields stretching across to the Welton Road Reservoir and Borough Hill.

Clarke's Farm is now St. Augustine's Way and the second rec is now a distant memory. In my early days the only house between London Road and Borough Hill itself was the Co-op Farmhouse behind the current Alan Pond garage. The white house on the ancient hill itself was built as a hostel for BBC workers.

Walking on Borough Hill at night in the early 1980s was an eerie experience, as you could clearly hear the 'World Service' broadcasts to those living behind the Iron Curtain, who were informed of what was really happening in the outside world. Polish, Russian, German etc were the languages of the day.

On the slip road up to the BBC Station was an old water tank, in which we children used to swim in as there was no pool in the town itself. All this came to an end due to tragedies in 1949 when five children were drowned, after getting into difficulty when bathing in the British Timken reservoir. Their graves are in the Holy Cross church cemetery. Abbey School Headmaster Hywel Hughes later organised a 'tote' competition which eventually raised the funds needed to build the outdoor pool at the bottom of the Braunston Road estate. A local farmer provided the land 'free-of-charge', and would have no doubt turned in his grave had he lived to see the Council close the pool to turn it into a car park. The site is still derelict to this day.

There were no damaging effects though when us children walked across to what is now Southbrook and climbed the iron bridge over the mid-19th century Weedon-Daventry-Leamington branch line. The more daring amongst us would then hang off the bridge, drop onto iron-ore trucks and hitch a free ride into the Daventry railway station. The trick was to jump out before the station master collared you!

Earlier memories were of attending Miss Hammond's Dancing school – a forerunner of modern-day Nursery Schools – in the old Abbey Buildings. There aged five I first met Mez Sommerton, who would eventually become my wife somewhile after she had lived and worked in London and abroad. We recently celebrated our Golden Wedding Anniversary.

Next up for both of us was then Ivymere Preparatory School in New Street, but this establishment was later closed overnight in scandalous circumstances. I moved onto schools in Old Bilton and Wellingborough, whilst Mez attended Northampton High School. Despite going to boarding schools I managed to maintain friendships with children of my own age, living in and around London Road.

My best friend John O'Shea sadly died at the early age of 42 years, but Hospital Matron's son Michael Punch was, like me, born in 1944, whilst the Hall, Thornton, O'Shea and Welch families all lived nearby in the Inlands. We spent hours playing in the South Brook which ran alongside the BBC Sports Field, which we never called Burton's Meadow.

Michael Punch's connection gave us free use of the hospital and its gardens, which then ran from London Road to what is now the Slade. Five full time gardeners were employed and it is a strange coincidence that I now live in The Dingle which once formed part of the hospital complex. I did tell you I hadn't gone far in life!

The use of the snooker room and the tennis courts were much appreciated, but my lasting memory is of a group of cell-like rooms attached to the northern end of this former workhouse in Victorian times. Anyone seeking a bed for the night had to earn their keep before being given shelter. Piles of big stones were put in each cell and had to be broken up and pushed through small grills before accommodation was provided.

Times moved on though and Daventry changed dramatically after World

War II. For a decade in the sixties Daventry was administered directly from Birmingham by Alderman Bowen (after whom the precinct is named). Faced with second City overspill, our Town Councillors handed over control of Daventry Council, whilst the equally affected Warwickshire town of Redditch refused Birmingham's advances.

Shopping changed to early supermarkets run by Masons and by Dick Newman (on Daventry High Street), were quickly replaced by Waitrose, Tesco, Aldi etc., as Daventry advanced towards the 21st century. As a sports buff though I was less than impressed by the absence of leisure facilities.

The excellently appointed Stead & Simpson's Sports Field, complete with football pitch, cricket ground, bowls club and dance hall disappeared because the Town Council failed to come up with the £30,000 needed to fend off the house builders.

Fords and British Timken also built Sports facilities which are no longer with us. The Town now has no cricket or hockey clubs, whilst the football and rugby teams operate from two of the worst pieces of marshland, Staverton Road and Stefen Hill, in the area. The land off London Road is now known as High March, Low March, Middle March, Broad March etc. This was a Council blunder as the street names referred to marshland and so should really be High Marsh and so on, not the 'Marches' which infers a border with Wales!

Badby Road no longer leads to Badby, Staverton Road doesn't go to Staverton... I could go on for ever but let's return to the positive. Daventry can now boast of the newly built Arc Cinema after losing the Regal (Bowen Square) and the Rex (Warwick Street) sometime around the end of the 1960s.

Other landmarks have also disappeared including the Grammar School, which was built in New Street in 1605, had relocated to North Street where it was still in use as a Comprehensive school when I first started teaching there in the mid-1970s. I can still remember driving down Sheaf Street, on into Brook Street and out into Braunston Road. The old bypass (now Western Avenue) actually went somewhere (the A45) and did not end, in a right angle as the current one does.

There is also something irrational about entering a town which has signs welcoming you to a 'historic market town'. From the South first impressions are of a scrap-car yard and a disused hotel. From the north you come across the ugly iCon Centre and a concrete jungle known as the Abbey Centre Retail Park.

Despite all this I truly love my home town, having lived here for nearly 80 years, and I am proud to live in a hugely under-rated area of upland Northamptonshire. Unlike the nearby Cotswolds, we do not have sight-seers gawping over our garden gates all summer, but some of our views are breathtaking. Try standing on the gated road to Preston Capes from Everdon Stubbs and looking back towards the village of Everdon itself.

What too about Fawsley Park, Weedon Barracks, the Country Park and the Braunston canal system? Daventry is also in possession of first-class communication systems. The M1. M40, Watling Street and the A45 are all within easy reach of a former boot and shoe town which now possesses high employment from diverse industries.

No doubt the conurbation will continue to grow and, after my lifetime, will join the town to Staverton, Badby, Welton, Braunston etc. By then my wife and I will have demonstrated our loyalty to Daventry having already paid for our burial plots in the Welton Road Cemetery.

Find us on

Thank you Daventry . . . for the Memories

Lawrence Wheeler pictured with Cheryl Thallon, owner of Sheaf Street Health Store at the launch of the Local Legends Wall